A TRIBUTE TO THE
REPTILES AND AMPHIBIANS
OF AUSTRALIA AND NEW ZEALAND

First published in 2019 by Reed New Holland Publishers
Sydney • Auckland

Level 1, 178 Fox Valley Road, Wahroonga, NSW 2076, Australia
5/39 Woodside Avenue, Northcote, Auckland 0627, New Zealand

newhollandpublishers.com

Copyright © 2019 Reed New Holland Publishers
Copyright © 2019 in text: The Australian Herpetological Society
and individual writers as credited
Copyright © 2019 in images: The Australian Herpetological Society
and individual photographers as credited

All rights reserved. No part of this publication may be reproduced, stored in a retrieval system or transmitted, in any form or by any means, electronic, mechanical, photocopying, recording or otherwise, without the prior written permission of the publishers and copyright holders.

A record of this book is held at the National Library of Australia.

ISBN 978 1 92554 659 0

Group Managing Director: Fiona Schultz
Publisher and Project Editor: Simon Papps
Designer: Andrew Davies
Production Director: Arlene Gippert
Printer: Toppan Leefung Printing Limited

10 9 8 7 6 5 4 3 2 1

Keep up with Reed New Holland
and New Holland Publishers
ReedNewHolland
@NewHollandPublishers and @ReedNewHolland

Cover photo: Northern Spiny-tailed Gecko
(*Strophurus ciliaris ciliaris*) by Jules Farquhar

A TRIBUTE TO THE REPTILES AND AMPHIBIANS OF AUSTRALIA AND NEW ZEALAND

THE AUSTRALIAN HERPETOLOGICAL SOCIETY

Edited by Chris Williams and Chelsea Maier

Contents

FOREWORD BY HAL COGGER	6
INTRODUCTION	10
THE CONTRIBUTORS AND EDITORS	11
FROGS AND TOADS	20
CROCODILES	50
TUATARAS	54
TURTLES	56
GECKOS	80
FLAP-FOOTED LIZARDS	122
SKINKS	126
DRAGONS	158
MONITORS	182
PYTHONS	198
FILE SNAKES	212
COLUBRID SNAKES	214
FRESHWATER SNAKES	220
VENOMOUS LAND SNAKES	222
INDEX	268
ACKNOWLEDGEMENTS AND REFERENCES	272

Etienne Littlefair photographing a Freshwater Crocodile.

PHOTO COURTESY CARA LITTLEFAIR.

Foreword

by Hal Cogger

The Australian Herpetological Society (AHS) started its long life in 1949 as the Australian Reptile Club. Founded by the late Roy Mackay, he brought together a group of about 25 enthusiasts from the Sydney area, organising monthly meetings at his home in Newtown and local field trips at weekends.

I joined the club as a 14-year-old in the hope of increasing my knowledge of local lizards and frogs and of learning how to catch, keep and study them. My concerned parents, puzzled by my eccentric interest in herpetology, were convinced that it was just a passing phase to be abandoned as soon as I discovered girls. It wasn't! And they also had no idea that snakes might also be caught and handled. Even my best school mates thought my interest in reptiles a bit weird.

I mention this background because the adult members of that club, who came from diverse backgrounds, became the best mentors an early teenager could have – not just in all aspects of herpetology but also as life guides. But to me it was the intensity of their interest in herpetology – while also going about their daily working and family lives – that convinced me that my own passion for reptiles and amphibians was healthy, acceptable and permanent. Some members even had partners who shared their interests!

The Australian Reptile Club morphed into the Australian Herpetological Society around 1951. Since those early days the members of the AHS have continued to maintain this critical mentoring role for new members and have, through their encouragement of young enthusiasts and their own field and captive studies and educational displays, been major contributors to knowledge and understanding of the distribution, ecology, systematics and husbandry of Australian reptiles and frogs. These contributions have been greatly extended through the society's constant stream of newsletters and now the impressive annual magazine *The Red Bellied Courier*. In 1963 the society published the first edition of the peer-reviewed scientific journal *Herpetofauna*, which in time was passed on to The Australasian Affiliation of Herpetological Societies who publish it to this day.

This book is a fascinating work on several levels, the most obvious being its representation of some of the diversity in colour, pattern and form to be found in the approximately 1,250 species of Australian and 120 species of New Zealand reptiles and frogs.

It is a gallery of outstanding photographs, each a credit to the patience, skill and imagination of the photographer.

Elliot Budd photographing an Inland Taipan.

PHOTO COURTESY JARI CORNELIS

Reptiles and amphibians are a challenge to any photographer. Like children, they are often unwilling to hold a pose. They will close their eyes, turn away from the camera and run or hop away just as the camera shutter is being pressed. In the wild one can look up from the camera after taking a picture and the subject is nowhere to be seen. I've even watched a kookaburra snatch a photographic subject sitting in front of me as I was composing its image on the camera's screen.

The images in this book also represent a time series in natural history photography that highlights the dramatic technical changes in cameras and photographic methods that have occurred during a single lifetime. From just 36 sequential shots on a single roll of ultra-slow (ISO 10) Kodachrome film to 1,000 or more continuous 50Mb digital images at ISO speeds of 6,000 or more, which was unimaginable even 20 years ago!

These technological advances have greatly expanded photographic opportunities and outcomes. Non-herpetological friends have returned from bushwalks with superb photographs taken on their mobile phones showing previously unrecorded behaviour in even well-known species of snakes and lizards. The photographic opportunities have never been greater.

Reptiles and frogs are widely recognised as critical indicator species in the conservation of both countries' biodiversity – critical in that they are the most abundant, accessible and resilient group of terrestrial vertebrates for study. Despite a number of them being seriously impacted by habitat loss and modification, no Australian continental or Tasmanian reptile species has become extinct since 1788.

The only reptile extinctions in the wild have been confined to a single island – Christmas Island – an Australian Territory that lies just below Java, and where the accidental introduction of the Oriental Wolf Snake (*Lycodon capucinus*) in the 1980s has in just a couple of decades brought three native skinks and a gecko – three of them endemic – to extinction in the wild. However, many mainland Australian reptiles and frogs remain equally vulnerable to the chance introduction of exotic predators or pathogens that could, like the wolf snake, or the chytrid fungus that has caused the decline or extinction of many Australian frogs, rapidly extinguish vulnerable species.

The best conservation tool is knowledge, and photography has a key role to play in building an effective conservation knowledge base. Great photographs of frogs and reptiles have been and will continue to be critical to alerting the broader community to their rich diversity and to their vulnerability to decline and extinction. This book engages the reader on many levels. I suspect and hope that it will also challenge the latent photographer that resides in most of us.

Etienne Littlefair
photographing a
Mertens' Water Monitor.

PHOTO COURTESY CARA LITTLEFAIR.

Introduction

Australia and New Zealand are blessed with a diverse range of reptiles and amphibians, and fortunately numerous books have been printed highlighting the myriad of species found in both countries. However, it is the people behind the camera who are responsible for bringing these animals to the readers and hobby enthusiasts, in the process often travelling huge distances to some of the most remote parts of both countries to locate the targeted species.

Finding the species, though, is only half the battle. The ability to capture a genuinely great image of a deadly snake, a lightning-fast lizard or a submerged turtle is a skill that very few people possess. In the era of digital cameras almost anyone can take a decent photo, but it is only a select few who have the patience, skill, technical ability and artistic flair to take one of truly remarkable standard.

The idea behind this book is to showcase not only the animals, but the photographers themselves. The Australian Herpetological Society has selected 25 of the most talented reptile and amphibian photographers to bring these unique and beautiful species to you. Each photo has its own detailed description of how the species was photographed and how the photographer managed to find and photograph it. Readers will be inspired by the variety of style each photographer brings to the species, and how seeing these animals up close provides a unique opportunity to appreciate the detail in their physical form.

The Australian Herpetological Society hopes that this book will inspire readers to begin or continue their passion for herpetology and/or photography. And also to continue to appreciate the natural beauty that both Australia and New Zealand hold in their lands.

Species names and taxonomic order

The species names and taxonomic order used in this book broadly follow those adopted by *Tadpoles and Frogs of Australia* (Second Edition) by Marion Anstis, *A Photographic Guide to Reptiles and Amphibians of New Zealand* by Tony Jewell and Rod Morris and *A Complete Guide to Reptiles of Australia* (Fifth Edition) by Steve Wilson and Gerry Swan.

Population status – the IUCN Red List

Established in 1964, the International Union for Conservation of Nature's Red List of Threatened Species has evolved to become the world's most comprehensive information source on the global conservation status of animal, fungi and plant species.

The IUCN Red List is a critical indicator of the health of the world's biodiversity. Far more than a list of species and their status, it is a powerful tool to inform and catalyze action for biodiversity conservation and policy change, critical to protecting the natural resources we need to survive. iucnredlist.org

EX Extinct
EW Extinct in the wild
CR Critically endangered
EN Endangered
EX Vulnerable
NT Near threatened
LC Least concern

THE CONTRIBUTORS

Shane Black grew up as a child in the bushy suburbs of south-east Sydney, making contact with reptiles from a young age. By the time he was in his early teens his main interest was elapids, the venomous snakes. By his early thirties, having kept and bred most of the large elapids, with some being the first instances of captive breeding for a particular species, photography and travel started to become his main focus. Soon after he relocated to far north Queensland and by that time the taipans had become his sole interest with regard to keeping, and also his main herpetological interest with regard to fieldwork and photography. He still travels extensively across the country in pursuit of photographing various species, with the tropics being his preferred regions. He currently lives in far north Queensland.
shaneblack71@hotmail.com

John Cann was born in Sydney in 1938 and has lived at La Perouse on the north shore of Botany Bay all his life. With brother George he ran the 'snake show' at La Perouse for 45 years, only passing it on in 2010 at the age of 72. John is recognised internationally for his pioneering work on Australian freshwater turtles, having discovered and described a number of species. He is an active advocate for their conservation and was awarded the Order of Australia (OAM) for Conservation, Environment, and Community in 1992. John has written a number of books on freshwater turtles and the history of Australian 'snakies'. His 1998 book, *Australian Freshwater Turtles*, remains one of the most highly rated and sought-after turtle books printed. The images presented here are a selection of those shown in that book, and in the later version printed in 2017.
johncann2036@gmail.com

Michael Cermak is a retired zoologist and wildlife photographer. Living and working with animals in north Queensland for four decades has given him a unique opportunity to build up an impressive photo library. He has MSc degree in Zoology and uses his knowledge and experience in his current profession as a nature photographer. Michael has published widely and is a regular contributor to several nature-oriented magazines and he has also published nine books. Although reptiles are Michael's favourite subject, he photographs other fauna from tiny invertebrates to large mammals in Australia as well as in many other places, including Sabah, Sarawak and Brunei in Borneo, Indonesia, Langkawi, Papua New Guinea, Madagascar, Japan and New Zealand. Understanding animal behaviour and ecology helps Michael to locate and approach (with his camera) many hard-to-find and -photograph species. Michael says: "Wildlife and landscape photography is a never-ending journey with no retirement plan."
michael-cermak.smugmug.com

Harold G. Cogger – better known as **Hal Cogger** – was born in Parramatta, New South Wales, in 1935, and acquired an intense interest in herpetology in primary school. He joined the Australian Reptile Club (the predecessor of the Australian Herpetological Society) at the age of 14, being encouraged by such great herpetological mentors as Roy Mackay, William (Bill) Hosmer and Alex (Rusty) Holmes. In 1952 he was appointed Cadet Preparator in the Exhibition Department of the Australian Museum in Sydney, then awarded a traineeship by the museum in 1954 to take him to the University of Sydney where he completed a Science degree (1955–58), returning to the Museum as Assistant Curator of Birds and Reptiles. He obtained his Master's degree by research in 1960, and was appointed Curator of Reptiles and Amphibians in 1963. In 1967 he was given part-time leave (1967–68) to complete a PhD at Macquarie University in its first teaching year. He returned to the Australian Museum in 1969, and was appointed Deputy Director in 1976. He retired in 1995 and was awarded an honorary DSc by the University of Sydney and for five years took up a part-time teaching post as Conjoint Professor at the University of Newcastle. He maintains an active research and publishing involvement in herpetology. He is married, with two children and four grandchildren. He has carried out extensive research and fieldwork in Australia, New Guinea and the Pacific Islands, and travelled to many overseas institutions to research the Australasian herpetofauna.
h.cogger@bigpond.com

Jari Cornelis has been interested in wildlife for as long as he can remember. He started by catching frogs and geckos with his dad in the garden in Gabon when he could barely walk. His parents could tell that he was passionate about nature and given a unique opportunity of travelling the world while growing up they always tried to incorporate visiting national parks, wilderness areas and zoos to fuel his interest. A trip to Australia at the age of 15 made Jari realise that he could turn his passion for wildlife into a career. There are not many places in the world where the fauna is so unique and the opportunities to study it are so great, so after high school he attended JCU for a Bachelor's in Zoology and Ecology and conducted a research project following that. This is where his interest in reptiles turned into an obsession and he began photographing them. He is currently studying Tiger Snakes for his Master's degree.
jari.cornelis@gmail.com

Scott Eipper is a herpetological consultant, author and wildlife photographer who works with his wife, Tyese, in their business Nature 4 You. As part of his role, Scott conducts wildlife surveys, snake management training, emergency removals and educational displays. He loves getting out searching for all reptiles and amphibians but his passion is venomous snakes. He has written five books and numerous papers and articles on Australian herpetofauna. Scott started taking photographs of reptiles as a 10-year-old, using his father's Konica before saving up enough to buy his first SLR – a Nikon F55. Using slide film he remembers vividly the time that whenever you pressed the shutter it cost you a dollar! This, he believes, forced him to learn the rules of composition and light which he still uses now, although today due to the lack of cost per shot he likes to experiment with techniques that go again those same traditional rules – with mixed results.
Admin@wildlifedemonstrations.com

Jules Farquhar says: "When people ask me, 'So, why reptiles?' my answer is simple: 'Just look at them'." From the moment he saw his first wild Mountain Heath Dragon he was forever enthralled by their appearance and behaviour. Documenting the beauty and diversity of reptiles and amphibians through photography has been a useful means of exploring this passion, which has taken him across Australia in search of herpetofauna to photograph and marvel at. During this time spent crawling around in the outback for elusive squamates it dawned on him that their ecology – not strictly the animals themselves – was equally interesting and worth investigation. And so, through the relentless pursuit of herpetofauna came sharper ecological awareness, and the floodgates opened into the world of scientific inquiry. With his interest in reptiles geared towards science, he decided to complete a bachelor's degree in Ecology, during which he developed a strong interest in research. He went on to investigate the post-fire response of reptile assemblages in Mallee Spinifex communities of arid New South Wales, and his current research investigates the factors limiting skink distributions in eastern Australia. He says: "Perhaps one day my interests will expand to be more inclusive of other vertebrate groups, but I highly doubt it."
jules-farquhar26@hotmail.com

Lachlan Gilding started his career with wildlife at the age of 15 when he secured an internship with a large zoological facility in southern Queensland. From then on he dedicated his life to wildlife conservation. After gaining experience for five years in the wildlife husbandry, training and conservation industry, he made the move into ecology and gained some valuable experience in the field, including travelling around the country and sometimes across the world to take part in some fantastic and unique conservation projects, from studying Womas in south-west Queensland to tracking Burmese Pythons in Bangladesh. In 2014, with the help of his close friend Max Jackson, he started a company called Australian Wildlife Encounters, which began by offering wildlife demonstrations, snake-handling courses and first-aid training, but soon evolved into offering wildlife tours. These days his tours take him to all corners of the country in the company of budding wildlife photographers, naturalists and natural history enthusiasts, in search of some of Australia's rarest and most unique fauna species.
Australianwildlifeencounters@gmail.com

Ken Griffiths became interested in reptiles at a very early age, since the days when if you wanted a pet lizard or snake then you just went out into the bush and caught one. Over the years he has kept a wide variety of reptiles but his favourites were always the local species that he could keep outdoors in natural conditions. He never kept large numbers – quality rather than quantity was always better. He also began taking photographs at an early age and bought his first SLR camera soon after he started working. During the years that followed he began finding ways to sell his images and eventually started placing his pictures with photo agencies in both Australia and the UK. At the time there was a good demand for Australiana photos and not all that many people supplying them. As he became more competent and experienced he started selling more images which eventually provided him with a steady income for many years. He also wrote and published some small field guides including *Frogs and Reptiles of the Sydney Region*, with several editions being produced. In more recent times he only keep a handful of local lizards and a few species of pythons, his favourite being the Diamond Pythons that he usually breeds most years. He enjoys keeping this species due to its docile nature and lovely colours. These days he is even more active with wildlife photography, something the digital age has made a lot easier, although this has also meant a lot more competition for getting images published.
kengriffiths@live.com

Jiri Herout is a photographer based in Sydney, who aims to portray the beauty and emotions of his subjects through imagery. He specialises in wildlife photography, landscapes and events and has been honing his techniques for more than two decades since he first picked up a Flexaret camera at school. He quotes the old adage that: 'You do not make a photograph with just a camera. You bring to the act of photography all the pictures you have seen, the books you have read, the music you have heard, the people you have loved.' And this is reflected in Jiris' images, which are full of emotion, love, beauty and energy.
hari@jiriherout.com

Max Jackson has dedicated both his career and his spare time to Australia's native wildlife. Over the past 10 years Max has accumulated a professional background in animal husbandry, wildlife consultancy, wildlife tour-guiding and conservation. He is also a passionate wildlife photographer who spends almost all of his spare time travelling across the country in order to find and photograph the unique species Australia has to offer.
australianwildlifeencounters@gmail.com

Tony Jewell was born in January 1976 and raised in Riverton on the southern coast of New Zealand's South Island. He became interested in herpetofauna from an early age and was fortunate to grow up in a region that was poorly explored in terms of its native lizards. This afforded much opportunity to explore blank spaces on the map, and in doing so record many new range extensions and previously unknown species. Highlights have been helping rediscover the long-lost Tautuku Gecko of Southland, helping uncover a diverse lizard fauna in the alpine zone of Fiordland National Park, helping save the critically endangered Cobble Skink of the West Coast from imminent extinction, and helping uncover New Zealand's largest lizard diversity (in and around the mountains of North Otago). His over-riding passion remains for the lizards of southern New Zealand, and particularly for field survey and research into their diversity and conservation needs. Photography has been an integral part of his herpetological work, both as a means of collecting scientific data and as an aid to help inform and inspire others. After stints living in Central Otago and Queensland he is now back on the south coast, in Invercargill, with his wife Anita and sons Baden and Bevan.
rocknvole@hotmail.co.nz

Chris Jolly is an ecologist living in Darwin, Northern Territory. He has broad interests in Australian natural history and conservation, with specific interests and expertise in Australian herpetofauna. Chris has been employed as a consultant herpetologist across Australia for his knowledge of reptiles. He is a dedicated wildlife photographer with a vast collection of Australian reptile photographs, with a particular focus on the reptiles of the Northern Territory. Chris is currently a University of Melbourne PhD candidate studying the behavioural and evolutionary consequences of conserving endangered species on islands. He has authored scientific journal articles on topics including herpetological natural history and ecology, invasive species impacts, conservation, evolution and behavioural ecology, many of which have been published in eminent international scientific journals.
cjol6201@uni.sydney.edu.au

Etienne Littlefair has had a lifelong interest in herpetology and the natural world. He achieved his Bachelor of Science with Honours in Zoology and Conservation at Bangor University, UK, and his Master of Science in Natural Resource Management from James Cook University, Cairns. He spent time working in ecological consultancy and for UK-based conservation organisations, with a strong focus on reptiles and amphibians, before moving to Australia. Etienne has lived in Darwin since 2016 and currently works as science teacher He spends the majority of his free time in the bush observing nature. Sharing his experiences through photography began as a record-keeping activity and has blossomed into Etienne's current project: documenting the freshwater aquatic ecosystems of the Top End. A unique submerged perspective allows the capture of powerful images of seldom-seen species.
wildterritoryimages@gmail.com

Jason Luke was born in Sydney in 1973. From early childhood he had a strong fascination for nature and wildlife, spending most of his free time searching the backyard, school playground and local parks for insects, frogs and lizards. Jason grew up watching every wildlife documentary and reading every wildlife book he could get his hands on. Spending hours looking at images of mysterious creatures from all over the world, he developed a strong interest in marine life, reptiles, amphibians and animal behaviour. It wasn't until his late twenties that he bought his first camera and went on his first overseas trip to Indonesia. It was this trip that started a fascination with Asian herpetofauna, and soon after his return from Indonesia, Jason joined the Australian Herpetological Society. Through the society, Jason met like-minded people, attended many field trips and began his ongoing love and learning of wildlife photography. Mostly self-taught, Jason has continued to develop as a photographer, and although it is a hobby and one that he takes seriously, he far more enjoys the places it takes him to and the friends he's made through it.
imagewildlife@gmail.com

Ross McGibbon is a Perth-based herpetological photographer. He is fascinated by reptiles and the natural world they live in, and for him there is no activity more fulfilling than learning about these animals, travelling to where they live and photographing them in their natural habitat. Over the years Ross has come to realise that the popularity of birds and mammals far outweighs that of reptiles. This is because the majority of people fear and misunderstand reptiles – particularly snakes. Therefore, he uses his images as a medium to spread education and awareness about reptiles via his social-media platforms. He says: "If I can help the public to appreciate and understand these extraordinary animals to even a fraction of the extent that I do, then I will consider my efforts well rewarded."
"In the end we will conserve only what we love; we will love only what we understand" (Baba Dioum, 1968).
rmrphotography.com.au

Gunther Schmida has been interested in all forms of wildlife, but especially 'cold-blooded' critters, for as long as he can remember, and he kept local frogs and the only three species of reptiles that occurred around his hometown of Brunswick in northern Germany in his youth. At age 13 he saw his first Asian Water Monitor in a zoo, and learning that most species known at that time came from Australia, decided to move there. He arrived ten years later in 1965, and has lived and worked in every state and territory since, picking his jobs in construction by the areas he wanted to explore more closely. At age 18 he had also taken up photography, buying his first camera to specifically snap fish in aquariums. After coming to Australia, this expanded to underwater photography, and photography of reptiles, frogs and other wildlife, always trying to do his subjects justice. He also started writing about his favourite subjects for many magazines globally, and his articles were published in eight languages worldwide. He is also the author of nine books. His images can be found in more than 500 publications and on almost as many covers. Yet, he has always remained an amateur. For the past 33 years he has enjoyed living in the hinterland of the Gold Coast in south-east Queensland, sharing his property with his wife and 23 species of reptiles and 13 species of frogs that abound in the garden.
ggg32@bigpond.com

Peter Soltys describes himself as a simple man, born and raised on planet Earth. He was fortunate enough to grow up around nature and animals, and because of this his passion for wildlife grows stronger every day. He has worked in different jobs here and there across the globe but for the last eight years he has held on to a job that allows him access to the best photography equipment you can find. In his spare time, Peter likes to travel and explore as many wild places as his wallet allows him. He makes no money out of it, but his photography hobby helps him to keep his head sharp and to stay healthy and happy. His life goal is to visit as many places as possible to witness the most incredible reptiles and amphibians before his wife finds out how much money that actually costs.
peter.soltys@yahoo.com

Gary Stephenson was born and raised in Sydney's eastern suburbs where, despite the density of development, municipal parks proved to be a treasure trove for wildlife (and in parts they remain so today). Gary joined the Australian Herpetological Society (AHS) and through it began to volunteer at the Australian Museum in Sydney during school holidays. Volunteering in the herpetology lab led to an interest in taxonomy being developed and encouraged. Over time, opportunities arose to collaborate on several projects. Already having an interest in photography, field trips only whetted the appetite to do more. Gary has travelled over a large area of Australia and also to South-East Asia and Africa in pursuit of capturing images of wildlife, not just reptiles and amphibians. Of particular interest to Gary is the capture of reptiles and amphibians 'in situ', meaning with no or very little external influences to hopefully get that perfect image and also perhaps tell a story about the subject in its natural environment.
gary.stephenson_1960@hotmail.com

Ben Stubbs has had a passion for wildlife, particularly reptiles, from a young age. He works professionally with captive reptiles and amphibians and his spare time is spent out photographing as well as working as a snake-catcher in the warmer months. He has been photographing wildlife since 2017, initially purchasing a camera to get better photos of snakes when he was releasing them after removing them from properties. A project that initially began as an endeavour to get some 'better' photos has now taken on a life of its own, with his camera now rarely out of his hands. The majority of his herping is done around the Melbourne area with a select group of good friends, with a yearly trip up to Darwin. He hopes to broaden his horizons and get into some new habitats and find some new species in the near future. With all his images he attempts to capture not just the animal, but also its behaviour and habitat, in order to add to the photo and also create a bit more of a narrative behind the image. To achieve these kinds of images he generally uses a wide-angle lens which requires close-proximity interactions with the animals, so knowledge of the species is very important before attempting these shots.
Benstubbs13@gmail.com

Matt Summerville was obsessed with dinosaurs from day dot and remains a *Jurassic Park* fiend. It wasn't long before his love of scaly things had him catching lizards in the backyard. However, obsession and a crazy thirst for knowledge soon had him wrangling all types of creatures, big and small, harmless and not so harmless, scaly and slimy. Matt grew up in a small town on the mid-north coast of New South Wales, where he spent most of his time either riding his bike or out in bush chasing critters. Once he finished school he made the move to Queensland and a 'bromance' soon formed with a Kiwi called Dan – the person Matt still curses to this day for getting him into wildlife photography – which has led to hundreds of hours of pure frustration and plenty of grey hairs. Any herper knows the deal – spending all of his free time, holidays and money travelling all over Australia looking for that next elusive species. It seemed a natural progression from taking quick 'proof' shots to spending time and effort on creating better photographs to remember all of those amazing species. Today Matt lives in tropical far north Queensland and continues to feed his reptile addiction as Senior Reptile Keeper at north Queensland's largest wildlife park, where can be found imparting his knowledge and enthusiasm of reptiles to the next generation. He is also infamous among reptile enthusiasts because of his unshakeable love of all things *Pseudonaja*. His favourite thing in the world is still to be out in the bush, as far away from people as possible, chasing reptiles around the undergrowth.
m.summerville@hotmail.com

Steve Swanson has been under the spell of reptiles for about as long as he can remember. As a child growing up in Sydney, his weekends were spent climbing about on sandstone slopes in the bush, searching for reptiles in the company of likewise-obsessed school friends. Initially he kept and cared for the reptiles he brought home in a backyard enclosure, but Steve's direction soon shifted from keeping reptiles in captivity to observing and photographing them in their natural environment. Steve's passion for photographing reptiles stemmed from a desire to share their beauty and diversity with others. For many years he has traversed the continent in search of subjects for his camera. Steve has authored five books on Australian reptiles and his photographs appear in many books by other authors.
swansonsteve2010@gmail.com

Rob Valentic has been obsessed with herpetology for as long as he can remember. He has been both a prolific writer of articles and supplier of images for nature magazines and scientific journals for over three decades. Rob's images have featured in *National Geographic*, *Australian Geographic*, *Reptiles Australia*, *Reptiles Magazine* in the UK and *Reptiles USA* magazines, along with numerous wildlife books and field guides. In late September 2014, one of his Tiger Snake images was used on a limited edition coin medallion and another on a postage stamp, both issued by Australia Post. Rob's work is represented exclusively by a professional agency, the Nature Picture Library based in Bristol, UK. Rob's frequent travels throughout Australia and internationally have been a constant driving force throughout his life and have resulted in a huge, ever-growing collection of herpetological images. He is based on a farm on the outskirts of Melbourne, where he lives with his partner Kelly and their daughter Indigo, plus 20 or so pet elapids and a load of camera and camping gear.
www.gondwanareptileproductions.com/

Dylan van Winkel is an ecologist and conservationist with an immense passion for wildlife, wild places and photography. He has worked on a variety of different taxa and ecosystems but has a specialist interest in herpetology, particularly within the Melanesian, Polynesian and Australasian regions. He is currently based in Auckland, New Zealand, and in his current role is involved with wildlife surveys and impact assessments, applied management and conservation, mitigation and translocations and invasive species management. Combining a passion for conservation and adventure, Dylan has travelled to several remote locations in the South Pacific, including Tonga, Papua New Guinea and islands off the coast of Tasmania, to carry out biodiversity assessments that have contributed to environmental protection initiatives. Another of Dylan's roles involves providing taxonomic determinations of foreign reptiles and amphibians entering New Zealand. He provides technical advice on herpetological incursion risk and eradications and maintains one of the world's most comprehensive databases and reference specimen collections of intercepted herpetofauna. Dylan is a contributing member of the New Zealand Lizard Technical Advisory Group and the IUCN Skink Specialist Group and is the lead author of *The Reptiles and Amphibians of New Zealand: A Field Guide*, published in 2018. His photographs have featured in numerous technical publications and books on a variety of natural history subjects.
dylan.vanwinkel@hotmail.co.nz.

Steve Wilson is a fauna consultant, an Information Officer with the Queensland Museum, a wildlife photographer and author. He has authored and co-authored nine books on herpetology, covering regional, state and Australian field guides, a natural history of lizards and a children's book. His images and articles are published widely in magazines in Australia and overseas. An award-winning photographer, he was nominated by *Australian Geographic* magazine as their 'Photographer of the Year' for 2000. Steve's interest in natural history and photography has led to extensive travel across Australia and to many of the worlds' unique biodiversity hot-spots.
stevekwilson@yahoo.com

THE EDITORS

Chelsea Maier is an environmental research scientist and herpetology hobbyist. She has been catching and keeping reptiles since she could walk. While attending university in the USA, she was lucky enough to spend a summer working with Dr Louis Guillette researching fight or flight responses in the American alligator. She dreamed of coming to Australia because of the unique reptiles and amphibians that the country has to offer, and made the journey over in 2011. She joined the Australian Herpetological Society in 2016 and soon found herself working as a committee member. She has worked on many volunteer-based projects involving reptiles and amphibians since moving to Australia and continues to have a child-like enthusiasm for the hobby. She particularly enjoys creating habitat for herps in her backyard to help with conservation and as a way of keeping other critters from eating her veggies. Chelsea is honoured to be able to work on a project such as this one and hopes that it will bring more inspiration to the field of herpetology in Australia, New Zealand and beyond.
chelseamaier@gmail.com | chelseamaier.com

Chris Williams has been a member of the Australian Herpetological Society since 1985, and has held the position of President for several years. Having previously worked in the reptile departments of Taronga Zoo and the Australian Reptile Park, Chris left the field, although in later years he would own Snake Ranch – Australia's largest breeding facility for reptiles, which is aimed at hobbyists specializing in python morphs. Chris is a passionate and prolific collector of reptile books, and through an admiration of seeing reptiles in print the idea for this book was born. Until now many of our best and most talented photographers were not recognised outside the social media bubble. Chris felt that this book was a way not only to highlight some of the amazing reptiles and amphibians that inhabit Australia and New Zealand, but also to give due credit to the people passionate about capturing their unique beauty for others to appreciate. Chris' third book, *An Illustrated Bibliography of Australian Herpetological Titles*, is due out later this year… as it was last year, and the year before that…
cdw460@gmail.com

SPECIES

Green and Golden Bell Frog (*Litoria aurea*)

PHOTOGRAPHER

Tony Jewell

STATUS

EX EW CR EN **VU** NT LC

LOCATION

Origin of specimen: Huntly, North Island

NOTES

Adult length up to 10cm. One of the few species active during the day. Sometimes found basking in the sun.

STORY BEHIND THE PHOTO

My interest in amphibians and reptiles began when I was only three years old. It happened one day when my older brothers, who had been out foraging for freshwater crayfish in one of the local streams at Riverton, in southern New Zealand, unexpectedly encountered an introduced Australian Southern Bell Frog (*Litoria raniformis*) and brought it home. Quite why I have no idea, but I was immediately captivated by this giant (to a three year old!) bright green frog. Yet, I was not allowed to touch it and it was soon released again. It was to be another six or seven years before I was to see another one of these frogs, for no matter how far and wide I searched I could not detect them anywhere. In the meantime I was finding the smaller Brown Tree Frog (*Litoria ewingi*) – another Australian import – and some native skinks, but it was the large green-coloured frogs which most fascinated and frustrated me. In these formative years my quest to find the mythical bell frogs grew into a maddening obsession. They were my favourite animal in the whole world, they lived right here in my home town, and nothing I tried could turn them up. When I had grown up a little, by about the age of ten, my green-frog drought suddenly broke. I had stumbled across an inadvertent artificial retreat among the emergent vegetation of a large pond, under which an adult male was sound asleep, and from that day on it was a simple matter to place sheets of tin and wood out in the bullrushes, and the frogs would gather. In the years that followed I kept them as pets, observed their behaviours in the wild, and mapped their distribution and habitat preferences across much of Southland. By the mid-1990s I had an outdoor colony in my Invercargill garden and would also spend much time observing them in the local ponds. Then, as the winter of 1997 came and went, the frogs vanished, both in my garden and in the wild. They had entered hibernation in seemingly good numbers, but would never again emerge. Chytrid disease had arrived and for the Southern Bell Frog it delivered a swift and total extinction in the far south. My favourite animal was, for the second time in my life, a ghost. Twenty years later I was doing some fieldwork near Huntly (in the North Island) and came across many dozens of the closely related Green and Golden Bell Frog (*L. aurea*) in swampy vegetation one night. Threatened by chytrid in its Australian homeland, this species is thriving in northern New Zealand and this encounter provided me with an opportunity to reconnect with my passion for Australian bell frogs. I took a small group home, and this photo shows one of the males soon after settling into its new habitat. I am glad to report that he and his mates have now taken over our glasshouse, where they earn their keep as full time pest controllers and plant fertilisers.

PHOTOGRAPHIC EQUIPMENT USED

Canon 400D, 900mm Tamron macro lens, f14, ISO 200, 1/100s with the pop-up flash.

SPECIES

Cape York Graceful Tree Frog (*Litoria bella*)

PHOTOGRAPHER

Jiri Herout

STATUS

EX   EW   CR   EN   VU   NT   **LC**

LOCATION

Northern Cape York Peninsula, north Queensland

NOTES

Average adult length c.4cm. This species remained unknown to science until recently and was first described in 2016.

STORY BEHIND THE PHOTO

The genus *Litoria* contains some of the most beautiful frogs, and in my opinion this species is one of the best. When I was lucky enough to see it in the far north of Queensland it was absolutely captivating. I found it on 30 May 2019, only relatively recently after it had been discovered and officially described. That day it had rained, so by evening there were a lot of frogs around. It was shortly after 8pm when we parked at the campground and suddenly I spotted big eyes on a small tree just right next to me an. It was *Litoria bella*.

This special frog lives mostly on trees near the rainforest waters of the northern Cape York Peninsula. It looks quite similar to the more widespread White-lipped Tree Frog (*L. infrafrenata*), with a beautifully coloured body in a shade of myrtle green, orange spots on the legs, purple thighs and a buttery yellow belly. I was so thrilled to see it and managed to take just two shots before it did a big jump and was gone.

The hunting strategy of these frogs is that they sit on tree trunks or branches, which gives them a better view of their prey. Females grow around 3.5–4cm and males are slightly smaller. This species is thought to feed predominantly on earthworms, flies, mosquitoes and other insects. Its presence adds to the beauty of this corner of north-east Australia and it was an absolute pleasure to see it in its natural habitat.

PHOTOGRAPHIC EQUIPMENT USED

Canon EOS 1DX Mark 2 with 100mm f/2.8L USM macro lens, which I find to be the best lens for small reptiles and amphibians as it is very sharp in recording tiny details. Canon 600 flash and two other external diffusers – one on the lens and the second on top of the flash so that the light was better dispersed – f20, ISO 100, 1/250sec. Focal length 100mm.

SPECIES

Eastern Dwarf Sedge Frog (*Litoria fallax*)

PHOTOGRAPHER

Ken Griffiths

STATUS

EX EW CR EN VU NT **LC**

LOCATION

Royal National Park, Sydney, New South Wales

NOTES

Tiny frog – maximum length only 3cm. A real survivor – one of the most common frogs on Australia's east coast, while in captivity individuals have lived more than 10 years.

STORY BEHIND THE PHOTO

These tiny frogs hide in the *Lomandra* clumps that grow along the banks of the Hacking River. They spend a lot of time basking high up in the leaves, but as you approach they quickly dive into the clump and disappear.

They can be a difficult frog to photograph in an in situ situation during the day due to their small size and wariness. Being so small, around 20–25mm, means that you need to use small apertures to get the greatest depth of field as possible. Going beyond f16 can be detrimental to the image as diffraction begins to appear, thus degrading the image. The way around this is to use a technique called focus stacking.

Basically a series of stepped photographs are taken from front to back of subject and then merged together in software to form a single image where the depth of field covers the entire subject area. This technique enables you to use the best aperture of the lens, which is about two or three stops down from wide open.

I used about 20 images to create this photograph. You have to be quick and take all the photographs in just a few seconds as any movement will ruin the shot and it has to be done again. It can be a tedious task but well worth it when it works.

PHOTOGRAPHIC EQUIPMENT USED

Canon 7D Mark 2, 100mm f2.8L macro lens, 1/200s, f8, ISO 500. I used focus stacking in this image to gain extra depth of field – a useful technique when photographing small subjects where depth of field is always an issue. The images were stacked using Adobe Photoshop CS6. Some cropping levels and sharpening was also used in the final output of the image.

SPECIES

Dainty Green Tree Frog (*Litoria gracilenta*)

PHOTOGRAPHER

Shane Black

STATUS

EX   EW   CR   EN   VU   NT   **LC**

LOCATION

Wonga Beach, far north Queensland

NOTES

Average adult length 4.5cm. Commonly found in orchards and banana plantations, meaning that stowaways are discovered in fruit shops across Australia.

STORY BEHIND THE PHOTO

The Dainty Green Tree Frog is found along the east coast of Australia. This particular specimen was photographed one steamy February night in 2017. Whilst living at Wonga Beach I had been hearing a roaring chorus of frogs each night, celebrating the wet season and looking for mates. I decided to brave the hordes of mosquitoes and ventured into the long swampy grass towards the frenzied calling. I was hoping to get in and out before I lost too much blood to the ravenous mozzies. I should have known that it wouldn't go to plan...

As I approached and the frogs became aware of my presence, they all went silent in unison. Then I would have to patiently wait in the dark with my head torch turned right down until they felt comfortable calling again. I can tell you now that five minutes sitting in the tropical rain while covered head to toe in mosquitoes feels like an eternity. Eventually, after several waiting periods and much blood loss, the frogs began to relax and continue on their merry way.

Normally I try and photograph animals in as natural a setting as possible. And while I did get many shots this way, I noticed this one individual sitting on a rusty piece of steel. I thought that the wet rust could really add some nice colour to the image, and I purposely lowered the flashes, aiming for a more arty image. On cue, the frog went quiet and refused to call for some time, testing my patience (which I'm not blessed with) to the limit. Just as I was about to give up and seek refuge from the humidity and blood-sucking insects, he started calling vigorously. I took a series of shots with the main aim of getting an image with his vocal sac fully expanded. Once I was confident I had the shot I wanted, I called it a night and headed back home.

I was pleased with how it turned out, and to this day it remains one of my favourite frog images, and well worth the mozzie blitz.

PHOTOGRAPHIC EQUIPMENT USED

Nikon D800 body, Nikkor 105mm macro lens, f22, 1/250s, ISO 100. Dual speedlights on a Manfrotto bracket utilised.

SPECIES

Heath Frog (*Litoria littlejohni*)

PHOTOGRAPHER

Peter Soltys

STATUS

EX   EW   CR   EN   **VU**   NT   LC

LOCATION

Central Coast, New South Wales

NOTES

Average adult length 5.5cm. Despite its reasonably large distribution this species is rarely encountered.

STORY BEHIND THE PHOTO

Cold and rainy winter nights are the best time to find this particular frog species. At the moment *Litoria littlejohni* is listed as 'vulnerable' due to habitat disturbance and the spread of the infamous chytrid fungus that is affecting its population. For a few years I had this shot in my mind but I was not sure how to obtain it. I had to keep in mind that photographing these frogs underwater in amplexus will require a lot of work, habitat research and an extreme amount of luck.

One of the main objectives was not to disturb the habitat and the frogs, in order to ensure that they could breed and produce a good number of tadpoles. I had to make sure that my boots and the underwater housing that holds the camera gear was perfectly clean from any oils, salt and other chemicals. I cleaned my camera gear with a mixture of bleach and water. After the preparation and gear disinfection I was ready to head out.

I knew that setting up the camera was another challenge as underwater photography has different rules. It took me a while to figure out what settings to use as my light source was not the strongest due the amount of diffusion and the size of the light. It had to be very portable. I had to place continuous light above the water level to reach the desired effect. Another alternative was a strobe mounted on top of the camera, however the effect would not be the same. Using continuous light was difficult, but so worth it.

Now, all I had to do is find the happy couple. It did not take long and they were very cooperative. It looked like they were not bothered by my presence at all. After a few shots I realised that autofocus would not be an option. I was photographing the frogs while it was raining and the water wasn't the clearest. Also, trying to get a wide-angle shot? Not sure what I was thinking, but luck was on my side. I took more than 300 shots and managed to get maybe two that I was happy with. Yes, this is still luck. If I consider the weather conditions, not being able to see the screen, and working without autofocus while using f4.5, I think I was more than lucky.

PHOTOGRAPHIC EQUIPMENT USED

Canon EOS 5D Mark III, Canon EF 24mm L Mark II f1.4, Aquatech Underwater Housing, LED light panel 1x1, f4.5, ISO 4000, 1/125s. Edited using Lightroom Classic.

SPECIES

Javelin Frog (*Litoria micobelos*)

PHOTOGRAPHER

Matt Summerville

STATUS

EX EW CR EN VU NT **LC**

LOCATION

Koah, Queensland

NOTES

The smallest Australian tree frog – rarely exceeds 2cm in length, with average length even smaller.

STORY BEHIND THE PHOTO

This particular frog was found on 11 January 2014, right in the middle of north Queensland's wet season, when it tends to rain most days and almost every night. When I moved to the wet tropics I was never really interested in frogs, but I quickly corrected the error of my ways, and spent many a night out trudging around in the rain, listening to calls and making the effort to see every frog species that the north has to offer – and there are a lot.

This particular wet and steamy night I headed out to a local pond that absolutely goes off with frog activity after a good downpour, and it's not uncommon to see ten species of frogs in one quick walk around the swimming pool-sized pond. My target for the night were Javelin Frogs, which are a tiny species, not much bigger than your fingernail, with a serious call. I wanted to get a photo of a male actually calling, but for a long time they were way too clever for me and would deflate their throat sacks as soon as they even sensed that a camera was in their vicinity. Until I stumbled across this little guy – he was the outcast – well away from the main body of water, all alone, calling his little heart out from between two blades of grass in a drain full of rubbish next to the road. This dude was on a mission, he was after the females, and no torch in his face or camera going off in close proximity was going to stop him from reaching his goal.

I snapped a bunch of photos until I managed to get a shot of his throat fully extended, showing all the lady frogs what he's all about. Even as a stood up, tripped, and dropped all of my camera gear right next to him he never missed a beat. This photo cost me my macro lens though, as it went for a swim in this little frog's drain. It was totally worth it for such a great little frog, and I definitely didn't get angry and storm back to the car. In hindsight it was a blessing in disguise.

PHOTOGRAPHIC EQUIPMENT USED

Nikon D610 with a (now deceased) Tamron 90mm macro. Edited in Lightroom.

SPECIES

Kuranda Tree Frog (*Litoria myola*)

PHOTOGRAPHER

Scott Eipper

STATUS

EX   EW   **CR**   EN   VU   NT   LC

LOCATION

Kuranda, Queensland

NOTES

Females average 6.5cm, males rarely exceed 4.5cm. Known to live in a tiny area near Cairns, and population thought to number less than 1,000 animals.

STORY BEHIND THE PHOTO

These frogs were found at an undisclosed location near Kuranda and the image shows a pair in amplexus. The reason for the secrecy is due to the sensitive status of this species, which is currently classified as critically endangered. The Kuranda Tree Frog is an example of a cryptic species – a species that remained undetected as a different taxon until call analysis and genetic sequencing uncovered it as a distinct species compared to the much more wide-ranging but morphologically identical Green-eyed Tree Frog (*Litoria serrata*).

This image was taken on a warm wet night near Kuranda. There had been a heavy downpour earlier in the afternoon and a brief shower as I left the vehicle to descend into the rainforest at dusk. I was walking up a stream in the forest when I came across a group of calling Kuranda Tree Frogs.

The call of *myola* comprises rapid clicks in short bursts, sometimes with a noticeable pause in between, and quite unlike the long drawn-out call of *serrata*, which has a slower tapping without the pause. Where their distributions overlap it is obviously important to find the frogs calling in order to determine the identity of the species you have located.

The tiny males are about one third the size of the females and they call from vines, rock faces and plants above or adjacent to rainforest pools. Initially this male was calling from rock when this large female approached him from the pool. His calling intensified and he jumped towards her and clambered onto her back, gripping just behind her forelimbs in a position known as axilliary amplexus. His distended vocal sac retracted as he pushed his chin in between her shoulders. As she turned on the moss-covered rock and faced back towards the water, I leaned over from my position in the muddy pool. I got one shot, annoyingly cutting off the edge of the knee and a toe before she hopped onto a low palm leaf. The powerful jump of the female made it apparent why it was so important for the small male to have such a tight grip.

I took a couple more photographs before the pair disappeared into the rainforest to complete their amplexus.

PHOTOGRAPHIC EQUIPMENT USED

Nikon D300, 105mm Sigma 2.8 DG macro, three SB 800 speedlites metered with ETTL, f20, ISO 200.

SPECIES

Roth's Tree Frog (*Litoria rothii*)

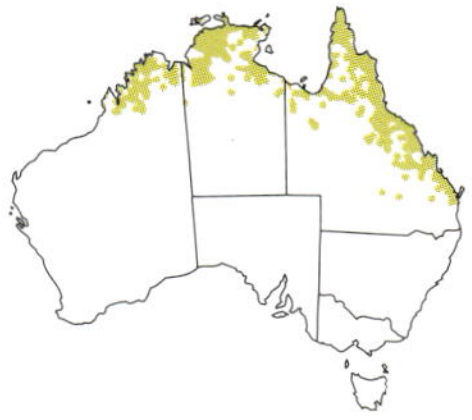

PHOTOGRAPHER

Jiri Herout

STATUS

EX   EW   **CR**   EN   VU   NT   LC

LOCATION

Cooktown, Queensland

NOTES

Can grow to an impressive 5.7cm. Able to alter its colour from pale grey during the day to dark brown after dark. Notably slow growth rate with females at higher altitudes not reaching sexual maturity until around four years old.

STORY BEHIND THE PHOTO

During one of our nights herping up in Queensland, we stopped at a rest area in a small national park near Cooktown. This was at about 9pm on 13 April 2018. As always, I was immediately looking for reptiles and amphibians. We had to be cautious as there was a pond inhabited by Saltwater Crocodiles nearby. After spending some time searching, I came across a frog sitting on a large eucalyptus tree. There was no doubt about the identification as it had one the most beautiful big purple-and-white eyes, which were looking straight in my direction. Roth's Tree Frog – it was love at first sight!

The colour of these frogs varies from quite pale to dark-spotted brown. Adults grow up to 5cm long. Breeding starts in the rainy season, whenever the main rains arrive after winter. I find it very interesting that the male can crawl up to 2m onto a tree overhanging water in order to call for females during the breeding season.

PHOTOGRAPHIC EQUIPMENT USED

Canon EOS 1DX Mark 2, Canon 600 Mark 2 flash and two other external diffusers – one on the lens and the second one on the top of flash so it dispersed the light – f13, 1/250s, ISO 100. Focal length 100mm.

SPECIES	STATUS
Spotted Tree Frog (*Litoria spenceri*)	EX EW **CR** EN VU NT LC

PHOTOGRAPHER	LOCATION
Rob Valentic	North-eastern Victoria

NOTES

This species can grow to 60mm. The species is regarded as extremely rare and has only been found in three locations along streams within Kosciuszko NP.

STORY BEHIND THE PHOTO

In mid-December 2012, my partner Kelly and I went on a trip into the high country of north-eastern Victoria specifically to locate and photograph *Litoria spenceri*. I had filmed this beautiful threatened species in 2004 using an analog film SLR but, due to the rapid rise in the quality of digital files, I wanted to shoot it with my new Canon DSLR while that was still an option in light of its uncertain future.

We arrived at the mountain stream that afternoon, setting up camp nearby. I noticed some ominous black clouds as I put the billy on but wasn't expecting the sudden, intense storm that battered and then destroyed our tent. After an hour the storm subsided but the temperature had plummeted. We decided to throw the jumbled mess back into the car and head home to dry out. As we departed I stopped the car at a feeder tributary and, already soaked, waded into the icy water for a brief last look.

The stream was running quite fast. I noticed an exposed shingle bed on the opposite bank that was overlain with several fist-sized stones that had evaded the rising water. Upon turning the first stone I was both shocked and exhilarated to see this magnificent adult male Spotted Tree Frog crouched beneath it. I could not believe my luck, as it often requires maximal and prolonged effort to locate the species and I had only ever found recent metamorphs in these situations before. I always conceal my right hand within a freezer bag as a glove for moments like this. I gently plucked the frog and reversed the bag, restraining him temporarily.

I set up my 240-volt petrol-fed generator that I use solely to run my set of studio lights, while Kelly put up the lights and stands next to a fallen log nearby. I then grabbed a cake-baking tray that I would use to create a miniature stream using stream gravel, some larger stones, riparian tussocks and creek water. The camera was mounted on a tripod and coupled to a vintage Leica bellows unit and lens, which produces images of exceptional detail and clarity.

In order to convey the laminar flow of the stream sections the species typically inhabits I used a slower shutter speed and asked Kelly to gently tap the edge of the baking tray to illicit water motion in the image. I then placed the frog on the stone in the centre of the tray using the freezer bag. I was so relieved when it posed beautifully for several shots. Within a few minutes he was promptly returned to the stream bank.

I was elated, exhausted, wet and cold as we packed up the substantial gear required to produce this shoot, but drove home so satisfied. A huge shout out to Kelly, who has always supported me unwaveringly.

PHOTOGRAPHIC EQUIPMENT USED

Canon 5D Mark III DSLR coupled to a vintage German Leica R Series Bellows rail system and 100/4 Leitz Wetzlar Macro Bellows lens from the late 1970s with a third-party adapter, Benro tripod, set of Elinchrom DLite4 IT Studio Strobes with skyport hotshoe transmitter, 240-volt Yamaha Unleaded Petrol Portable Generator and lead. Adobe Photoshop Elements 2018 with Raw plugin.

SPECIES

Orange-thighed Tree Frog (*Litoria xanthomera*)

PHOTOGRAPHER

Steve Swanson

STATUS

EX EW CR EN VU NT **LC**

LOCATION

Lake Eacham, Queensland

NOTES

Averages about 5.5cm in length. Congregates and breeds in ponds in dense rainforests. Up to 1,600 eggs can be produced from a single female at one time.

STORY BEHIND THE PHOTO

I have a small, constructed pond at the front of my house at Lake Eacham on the Atherton Tableland, and each year two species of frogs make use of it for breeding: the Northern Stony Creek Frog *(Litoria jungguy)* and the Orange-thighed Tree Frog *(Litoria xanthomera)*. The Orange-thighed Tree Frogs appear at the pond immediately following the first heavy rain of the season, and it is not unusual for 10–15 individuals to gather and call in and around the pond. They announce their arrival with a loud 'waark, waark' call. At times their multiple calls create such a cacophony that I need to close the windows in order to be able to hear the TV.

The Orange-thighed Tree Frog is an attractive and photogenic species, and the various interactions of the individuals at my pond provide many photographic opportunities. I walked about ten paces from my front door and snapped this photo one night in December 2016.

PHOTOGRAPHIC EQUIPMENT USED

Pentax K10D, Pentax 90mm macro lens, f19, flash sync speed 1/180s. External flashgun mounted on camera hotshoe. Some minor adjustments to the image using Photoshop.

SPECIES

Western Spotted Frog (*Heleioporus albopunctatus*)

PHOTOGRAPHER

Matt Summerville

STATUS

EX EW CR EN VU NT **LC**

LOCATION

Jurien Bay, Western Australia

NOTES

Reaching lengths of 10cm, this species spends long periods underground during the warmer months, emerging with the rains to feed and breed.

STORY BEHIND THE PHOTO

Towards the end of November 2019, myself and a couple of good mates were just wrapping up a whirlwind road trip around southern Western Australia where we'd experienced every type of weather imaginable – most of which was cold – and we decided to hit an area near Jurien Bay that looked promising for a small elapid, a small elapid that just happened to be one of my favourite Australian snakes. Spoiler – we didn't find it. Not this night anyway.

As the sun set, and the mercury plummeted, the boys set out slowly cruising the roads and I walked the sandy trails through the heath country looking for any reptile activity. Secretly I was also desperately wanting to see a Honey Possum, which I also failed at. After many hours of unsuccessful searching, and the odd eye-shine of Cloudy Stone Geckos as they tried to suck the last bit of heat out of the rocks, I rounded the last bend that led back to where the guys were going to pick me up.

Up ahead I spotted two enormous eyes peering back at me from the bottom of the heath. Surely this was too big to be one of the giant ticks that any Western Australian herper knows about all too well? As I quietly approached I was greeted by one of the biggest frogs I've ever seen – it even rivalled some of the small dog-sized Cane Toads we get back home in the tropics. The only amphibian that was brave enough to make an appearance on a night where the temperatures had quickly dropped into the low teens, this glorious beast was the Western Spotted Frog – a new species for me. As I'm an avid frog enthusiast, I decided to get my knees dirty and took a souvenir photo of it before continuing on my way, happily trotting back to the car and excited to tell Greeny, as I knew he would share my excitement just as much, if not more, and it would surely relieve that sore point of not seeing a Bardick that night.

PHOTOGRAPHIC EQUIPMENT USED

Nikon D610, Nikon 60mm f/2.8 macro.

SPECIES

Desert Spadefoot (*Notaden nichollsi*)

PHOTOGRAPHER

Peter Soltys

STATUS

EX EW CR EN VU NT **LC**

LOCATION

Windorah, Queensland

NOTES

Females reach 7cm and like many species of frog are slightly larger than males. Spends the warmer months underground and emerges to feed and breed in the wet season. Tadpoles can go from birth to fully formed frogs in as little as 30 days.

STORY BEHIND THE PHOTO

If you ever manage to reach central Australia and you come across a *Notaden* frog, you know you are in the right spot at the right time. This frog comes out in numbers only during perfect conditions. It breeds after heavy rain in shallow desert depressions that become filled with water, and that does not happen very often in the remote Australian outback. Those perfect conditions occurred around Windorah in November 2016.

A trick to photographing this frog is that you have to be quick, and that is actually the case for most frogs. As soon as you take too many shots the frog gets stressed and it starts jumping around, or it tries to hide and dirt gets stuck on the skin due to all that moving about. I remember when I started frogging, I used to practice on small rocks and pebbles just to make sure I knew that my shooting angles and light/diffusion combinations were correct. Do not get confused by this frog's grumpy face – that is how they normally look.

PHOTOGRAPHIC EQUIPMENT USED

Canon EOS 5D Mark IV, Canon EF 100mm f2.8 L Macro IS USM, Canon speed light 600EX, f18, 1/160s, ISO 200. Combination of softbox and second diffusion. Flash setting – ETTL. Editing program – Lightroom classic.

SPECIES

Ornate Burrowing Frog (*Platyplectrum ornatum*)

PHOTOGRAPHER

Jason Luke

STATUS

EX EW CR EN VU NT **LC**

LOCATION

Yuleba, Queensland

NOTES

Reaches an average of 5cm in length. Common in relatively populated areas and often confused with the introduced Cane Toad.

STORY BEHIND THE PHOTO

This species is extremely common throughout most of its range. Although I have found them many times, even in the north-western parts of Sydney, they do not occur where I live in south Sydney. So when I have the opportunity I take the time to photograph them, especially as they vary highly in colour and pattern.

I took this image whilst away on a camping and herping trip with friends in the Brigalow area of southern Queensland in January 2019. We experienced heatwave conditions, with temperatures of more than 40°C by day and 30°C at night. Animals of every type were suffering and it was difficult to find signs of life in the parched landscape. We focussed our search mostly on areas close to water.

On this night we were in the Yuleba State Forest, driving the dusty dirt roads when at around 9.30pm we discovered a dry creek bed that had some stagnant pools of water remaining. A scan around with our head torches showed up some frog eye-shine so we left the cars and started walking down the creek bed to see what we could find. There seemed to a be a number of common frog species around, a sleeping Eastern Water Dragon and a small cave system with nine or more echidnas sheltering in it – most likely all trying to escape the heat.

This uplifted our spirits somewhat in what was looking like a tough night to find anything, so I decided to photograph a few frog species while we were here. I noticed some Broad-palmed Frogs (*Litoria latopalmata*) around one edge of the pond and was kneeling on the ground photographing them when I spotted a pair of eyes sticking out of the damp dirt, looking at me just a few inches away from my knee. I recognised them as belonging to an Ornate Burrowing Frog and was happy as I didn't have any in situ shots of them semi-buried. I was also happy that I hadn't knelt on the frog and I repositioned myself so that I could take some photographs. We ended up finding some nice snakes that night and I got some good photos of them. Even so, this image of the Ornate Burrowing Frog is one of my favourite shots of the night due to the circumstances in which I found it and the fact that the photo was taken in situ.

PHOTOGRAPHIC EQUIPMENT USED

Nikon D800, Nikon 105mm Micro, Nikon SB910 Speedlight, Lastolight Micro Softbox and Interfit Strobies Diffuser, f22, 1/160s, ISO 100, 105mm. Image adjusted on iPhoto.

SPECIES

Spencer's Burrowing Frog (*Platyplectrum spenceri*)

PHOTOGRAPHER

Chris Jolly

STATUS

EX   EW   CR   EN   VU   NT   **LC**

LOCATION

Simpson's Gap, West MacDonnell National Park, Northern Territory

NOTES

Reaching just under 5cm in length they are slightly smaller than their eastern cousin, the Ornate Burrowing Frog. Female lays around 1,100 eggs during the wet season, mostly in temporary pools of water.

STORY BEHIND THE PHOTO

This photo was taken in September 2016, during a trip to Alice Springs for the Australian Society of Mammalogists (apparently because I've done a PhD on mammals I'm a mammalogist, but I am still a herpetologist at heart). Central Australia had enjoyed a very wet start to 2016 and the birds, flowers and herps were going gangbusters. Because of this, instead of flying into Alice Springs we decided to drive the leisurely route from Adelaide to Alice via a remote property in the south-east corner of the Northern Territory to look for Letter-winged Kites – one of Australia's rarest and most nomadic raptors and one of the Holy Grails of Australian birding.

On the nights of the conference, instead of socialising and furthering my career as a scientist, I opted to go searching for frogs and reptiles in the areas surrounding Alice Springs. Within minutes of arriving at our intended herping site I started spotting what looked like frog eye-shine all over the base of the sandy, River Red Gum-lined, drying river bed. However, as I approached the eye-shine I could not see a frog. I assumed that my eyes were playing tricks on me and that I was actually seeing the eye-shine of minute spiders. Then I saw the same eye-shine again, but this time I was convinced that it belonged to a frog – but again no frog could be seen. This time I got down on my knees for a closer look and spotted two eyes amongst the grains of sand. They were frogs! They were burrowing frogs that were undecided on whether to come out or remain in their burrows. I thought it best to leave them to make that decision for themselves and took the photo while this one was still buried.

PHOTOGRAPHIC EQUIPMENT USED

Canon 7D, Canon 60mm macro, Twin Canon 430EX II speedlites and Adobe Lightroom.

SPECIES

Southern Gastric Brooding Frog (*Rheobatrachus silus*)

PHOTOGRAPHER

Hal Cogger

STATUS

EX EW CR EN VU NT LC

LOCATION

Frog from Montville, Queensland, photographed Turramurra, NSW

NOTES

There were two species of gastric brooding frog, the largest reaching 5.4cm. Sadly both became extinct in the 1980s. Their story and biology are fascinating yet tragic and deserve further reading.

STORY BEHIND THE PHOTO

This distinctive and now-extinct aquatic frog was first found almost within sight of the Brisbane CBD but was not formally described to science until 1973. The subsequent discovery, published in 1974 by Chris Corben, Glenn Ingram and Mike Tyler, that this frog incubated its eggs in its stomach, caused amazement and some disbelief among biologists as it was not only the first frog, but the first vertebrate in the world to display this mode of reproduction – how could the eggs and tadpoles of the frog survive and grow in the mother's stomach without being digested?

Although a second species of gastric brooder (*Rheobatrachus vitellinus*) was later (1984) described from upland rainforest in Eungella National Park, Queensland, it too apparently became extinct only a few years later – before its biology and ecology could be fully studied. Both species were among the vanguard of native frog species lost to the impacts of an exotic chytrid fungus (*Batrachochytrium dendrobatidis*) that had been unintentionally introduced into eastern Australian streams. Although I had the opportunity to see *Rheobatrachus silus* briefly in the wild, its shy nature within its aquatic habitat made it very difficult to find and photograph without adequate time, patience and specialised equipment, and so most photographs made of this species by herpetologists were of one of the few individuals maintained in biological laboratories.

This photograph was taken at home at short notice when a visiting herpetologist passed through Sydney with a live specimen. I set up a small aquarium for the frog using local stream water and stream leaf litter as substrate. A separate shot of rainforest stream-edge vegetation was taken and later added to the photograph's background solely for aesthetic and context purposes. While laboratory shots were also taken on plain, artificial backgrounds for strictly scientific illustration, this composite photograph has been used by many conservation agencies around the world to illustrate not only the frog's current conservation status but also its classical aquatic adaptations and general appearance. The subsequent extinction of this species has thus made this rough, makeshift composite image one of the most sought-after of my photographs and is a reminder that photographic quality, set in natural habitats, are not the only criteria determining the scientific and photographic value of an image.

PHOTOGRAPHIC EQUIPMENT USED

Photograph taken in September 1978 with a Leica 1G camera with mirror reflex housing attached and 65mm macro Leitz Elmar lens on Kodak 64 ASA Kodachrome film and with two flashes – one above the aquarium and the other at a high angle between the camera and the front glass of the aquarium to avoid reflections of either the camera or flash. Age and projection dust and scratches and dirt particles in the water were removed after scanning using Photoshop CS3.

SPECIES

Freshwater Crocodile (*Crocodylus johnstoni*)

PHOTOGRAPHER

Michael Cermak

STATUS

EX EW CR EN VU NT **LC**

LOCATION

Wangetti, north Queensland

NOTES

Males can reach 3m, females rarely exceed 2m. Much more timid than Saltwater Crocodile and not a danger to humans. Dwarf populations with individuals that rarely exceed 1m occur in Arnhem Land and around the Bullo River. Numbers were decimated by Cane Toads, yet the crocs have now adapted and appear to eat only the toads' back legs, thus avoiding the poison glands located behind their head.

STORY BEHIND THE PHOTO

This was an experimental shot that turned out quite well. In 2010 a friend of mine lent me his Canon 400mm f2.8 prime lens for an upcoming shoot on Cape York. It was a very generous gesture, especially considering that I had that lens in my care for the following five years. It travelled with me to many faraway places, including Madagascar in 2013 and Borneo the following year.

Of course, before any serious shooting, I had to give it a test run, so took it to Hartley's Adventures, an animal park just north of Cairns. That's where I took this shot of a Freshwater Crocodile resting on a log. I was keen to see what the subject separation and the bokeh would look like with the aperture set to f2.8 with this long lens. Even though I set a relatively high shutter speed (but low ISO), I rested the lens on a railing, held my breath for a second or two and pressed the button. I was pleased with the result.

The one disadvantage of this very expensive lens is its weight. Mounting it on my camera (with a battery pack) brings the total weight to whopping 7kg, so a sturdy tripod is a must. But that's not always possible or practical. On another occasion, I was shooting flying-foxes in flight with this gear hand-held. It was fun until my arms went numb and I was suffering from the effects of RSI for the next five days. After this experience I went and bough myself a monopod.

PHOTOGRAPHIC EQUIPMENT USED

Canon 1Ds Mark III, Canon 400mm L 2.8 prime lens, f2.8, 1/1000s, ISO 100.

SPECIES

Saltwater Crocodile (*Crocodylus porosus*)

PHOTOGRAPHER

Matt Summerville

STATUS

EX   EW   CR   EN   VU   NT   **LC**

LOCATION

Wujal Wujal in the wet tropics region of north Queensland

NOTES

The giants of the reptile world. Males can reach 6m, females are half that. Normally 25–30cm at birth, but attain lengths of 1m within a year, by which time only other crocodiles and large pythons pose a real threat. Unregulated hunting for their highly prized skins occurred until the 1970s, and it's estimated that 95 per cent of the population was wiped out during that time.

STORY BEHIND THE PHOTO

This photo was taken on 27 September 2018, along the Bloomfield Track near the indigenous community of Wujal Wujal, while just on a day-drive exploring paradise. We parked in the small car park next to the water, observed the croc warning signs, and walked in to check out a remote waterfall. Whilst walking along the creek I was of course keeping an eye out for crocodiles, which I never get tired of seeing in north Queensland, as they're nowhere near as common as cowboy-hatted wearing politicians make them out to be. Right in front of the waterfall there were a few people swimming in what looked to be a fairly deep hole – we'd found the owners of the van that was perfectly parked across three parking spots at the start of the track. Only 30m to their left, in clear view, was a big yellow crocodile warning sign of the type that are commonly used as towel racks in north Queensland, and 50m downstream from the sign, on the opposite side of the creek, this subadult Saltwater Crocodile was basking on a rock soaking up the last rays of sun for the afternoon.

She let me approach fairly closely, which is pretty uncommon for the crocs around this region as they're used to humans harassing them. Usually they dive into the water never to be seen again. Instead she slowly opened her mouth and sat like that for a couple of minutes as the clouds blocked out the sun. When the sun poked its head back through the clouds, I took a couple of photos and left her alone to keep soaking up the sun in peace.

Crocodiles are always among my favourite animals to see in the wild, and even though I've seen a lot of them it was still cool to see this animal that was relatively unfazed by humans sitting so close to a group of people that obviously had no idea she was nearby and meaning them no ill intent. As we walked back down the creek towards the car we passed a group of people heading in the opposite direction, towels in hand, proving that humans are the most intelligent species on the planet.

PHOTOGRAPHIC EQUIPMENT USED

Nikon D610, Nikon 80-400mm AF-S VR lens. Edited in Lightroom.

SPECIES

Tuatara (*Sphenodon punctatus*)

PHOTOGRAPHER

Jason Luke

STATUS

EX   EW   CR   EN   VU   NT   **LC**

LOCATION

Matiu/Somes Island, Wellington, North Island

NOTES

Length up to 80cm. These 'living fossils' resemble lizards but are in their own distinct group which flourished 200 million years ago, of which the Tuatara is the lone survivor. While listed as Least Concern, its survival relies entirely on active conservation management of the islands it inhabits.

STORY BEHIND THE PHOTO

The Tuatara is one of the world's truly iconic reptiles. It looks like a lizard, but isn't one. It is the last remaining member from an ancient group of sphenodontid reptiles – a living dinosaur if you will. So when the opportunity came to visit New Zealand for my honeymoon in November 2018, we booked two nights for a chance to see these amazing reptiles in the wild.

Unfortunately the Tuatara has suffered badly due to the introduction of various species including rodents. It was almost driven to extinction and only survived on a few remote islands. Recent breeding efforts and reintroductions have seen the species thrive on several more offshore islands, as well as in fenced sanctuaries and breeding facilities on the main islands. Two of these islands – Matiu/Somes Island in Wellington Harbour and Tiritiri Matangi Island near Auckland – are open for tourists to go and see them, living naturally in a rodent-free environment. We booked one night on each of these islands to cover our bases, staying in the Department of Conservation accommodation. Foul weather prevented us from getting to Tiritiri Matangi as the ferry service was cancelled. The night before we were due to go to Matiu/Somes Island, I sat in a Wellington hotel watching rolling waves and rain pelting sideways propelled by freezing gusts of more than 100km per hour. To say I was concerned is an understatement. There was a very slight improvement the following morning but it still looked terrible. Expected evening temperatures were below 10°C and wind and rain persisted. The ferries were running again by late morning so we made the decision to give it a go.

Even though I knew that Tuataras are cold-weather specialists I was still doubtful. That was until I met a Department of Conservation ranger who assured me that we would find some. Happy days! And find some we did. We set off after dark while it was still windy, raining and about 8°C. The loop around the island takes about 30–40 minutes to walk, and on each circuit we found four to six different Tuatara. Most were sitting out on the green lawn, which was not ideal for a photo. It was raining steadily and I wasn't keen on getting my camera gear out, so I went back to our accommodation and waited.

I ventured back out when the rain eased at around 10.30pm. I found a number of Tuatara again all sitting on the grass, so started to look more intently in the undergrowth where the grass wasn't growing. I eventually located one sitting in some exposed roots at the base of a small tree. I took a few shots of it before it clumsily disappeared down its burrow. I don't think I've ever been happier to get a photo. It was a real privilege to see the Tuatara and be able to photograph it – it is a truly amazing reptile species.

PHOTOGRAPHIC EQUIPMENT USED

Nikon D800, Sigma 24mm ART f/1.4, Nikon SB910 Speedlight with Lastolight soft box and Interfit Strobies Diffuser, f16, 1/250s, ISO 160, 24mm. Image adjusted using iPhoto.

SPECIES

Sandstone Long-necked Turtle (*Chelodina burrungandjii*)

PHOTOGRAPHER

Etienne Littlefair

STATUS

 EX EW CR EN VU NT **LC**

LOCATION

Arnhem Land, Northern Territory

NOTES

Carapace length averages around 30cm. At first glance appears similar to other species of long-necked turtle, and this may have led to its misidentification until closer examination. Formally identified as a distinct species in 2000.

STORY BEHIND THE PHOTO

This photo was taken on 4 April 2018 shortly after 10pm. This nocturnal species, which is also known as the Arnhem Land Long-necked Turtle, has a disjointed and uncertain distribution. It is primarily known from the sandstone escarpment creeks of Arnhem Land and the Kimberley region of Western Australia.

Having seen and photographed the Kimberley population, I set my sights on locating a Northern Territory specimen closer to home and from the area whence the species had been described in 2000. Before entering the water at night, my wife Cara and I staked out various small, clear water bodies during the day, watching carefully for turtles coming up for air. We did this in a remote region to the north-east of Katherine. We wanted to be sure that we had the correct species of turtle and a complete absence of Saltwater Crocodiles, and we had excellent local advice regarding the Saltie situation. Within two days of searching we had found our spot, and even briefly observed our quarry during a daytime snorkel session – a rare treat in warm Top End waters.

Before I entered the water after dark, I knew I wanted a photo that clearly showed the key features of the turtle, but also captured the eeriness of black water so that viewers would be left in no doubt that they looked upon a nocturnal species. After nearly an hour of slow careful swimming I was nearly ready to give up and call it a night when this turtle emerged from a deep pool beneath me and swam straight past me and up the bank for a breath of air – this brief encounter provided all I needed to capture the image I had hoped for. Leaving the water, I knew we had succeeded in our mission; other times it has taken my wife and I many attempts to achieve such results with aquatic species. We were overjoyed and, to boot, we had spotted a Saw-shelled Turtle, giving us good reason to return.

PHOTOGRAPHIC EQUIPMENT USED

Olympus EM1 Mark II, Olympus 7–14mm f2.8 lens, Nauticam housing, Sea and Sea strobes. Processed using Adobe Photoshop CC.

SPECIES

Broad-shelled Long-necked Turtle (*Chelodina (Macrochelodina) expansa*)

PHOTOGRAPHER

Gunther Schmida

STATUS

EX   EW   CR   EN   VU   NT   **LC**

LOCATION

South-east Queensland

NOTES

Female typically larger than male and can attain carapace length of 50cm and weigh up to 6kg. Reaches sexual maturity at around 10 years for male and 15 years for female.

STORY BEHIND THE PHOTO

Turtles can be photographed in different ways. In the wild, by using a long telephoto lens to capture them basking, or using an underwater camera to take shots in situ. The first method is relatively easy and just requires knowledge of where to find turtles and how to use a long lens effectively. Underwater photography involves much more. Apart from knowing turtles well, it also requires some fitness, and some pretty sophisticated equipment. Good underwater shots also need very clear water, and one needs to get very close to a subject to be successful. Finding suitable habitats that meet all criteria is the largest hurdle. Another way to photograph turtles is to stage the shots. This is no big deal if taken out of water, but in water it is a different story. I have tried all methods and found the latter to be the best for creating the images I wanted.

I had photographed freshwater fish in aquariums for some time when 'turtle man' John Cann persuaded me to try my luck with his turtles. At first I could not warm to it, but now turtles are some of my favourite subjects. Over the years I have learned a lot about turtles while trying to get in-water pictures of almost all known Australian species and their forms. Some were easy, others difficult. I use large aquariums with powerful filtration and create habitats as close to nature as possible.

Most turtles need time to settle, so if they have already been kept in aquariums the battle is half won. This was the case with these two Broad-shelled Long-necked Turtles. They had been picked up as hatchlings on a road near Beenleigh, south-east Queensland, during heavy overnight rain. The locals who found them had no idea what they were but thought they looked cute, so took them home. To their credit they looked after them well, feeding them natural foods and moving them into larger tanks as they grew. After two years however, the owners were moving overseas and looking for a new home for their critters. That is how I ended up with them, albeit briefly before they went to a new owner.

The shot was taken in my 1,500 litre tank that is specially designed for photographing larger subjects. The image was illuminated with 12 flashguns, including nine small studio flashes from above to light the scene as evenly as possible, and two small studio flashes at low level, mounted at front on each side of the tank to lighten the lower sections. Lastly, the master at half power, also mounted at the front on the same level as the guns on top of the tank but a metre from the front glass and angled downwards towards the inside. Only the master was connected to the camera, all others are triggered by in-build slaves.

I sat back about 2.5m from the tank waiting for some action. The turtles took no notice of me.

PHOTOGRAPHIC EQUIPMENT USED

Nikon D300 DSLR, Micro Nikkor 70/180mm set on 70mm. f16, duration of synchronised flashes 1/1000s, ISO 400. Image cropped by about 25 per cent in Photoshop CS5.

SPECIES

Snake-necked Turtle (*Chelodina longicollis*)

PHOTOGRAPHER

Gunther Schmida

STATUS

EX EW CR EN VU NT **LC**

LOCATION

South-east Queensland

NOTES

Carapace length around 28cm, though smaller for males. Animals in certain locations can have smaller average size. When threatened the defence is to emit a fluid from its musk glands which is offensive to other living creatures, with the exception of other Snake-necked Turtles, and herpetologists.

STORY BEHIND THE PHOTO

I had wanted to photograph a hatchling Snake-necked Turtle since I had taken up 'in-water' turtle photography well over 30 years ago, but for some reason it had just never happened.

Then Brian Furry McLean, well-known reptile enthusiast, showman and musician, came to the rescue by supplying a captive-bred hatchling just a few days old, for me to try my luck. Thanks Brian.

It was photographed in a fully aqua-scaped 180-litre tank to get as natural looking shots as possible. This image was illuminated with four small studio flashes mounted above the tank, with the master in front at the same level and about 50cm in front of the glass and angled about 45° down.

Then it was just a case of waiting and observing until the right moment arrived. Turtles cannot be manipulated. Over time I have learned when to point the lens at my subjects and that was the case here. This image is my best example to explain the importance of focusing on the eyes. I do not use autofocus, rather move to and fro as required. If the eyes look sharp the rest does not matter. There will always only be a certain depth of field anyway, especially in close-up photography.

Judging by the number of times that this shot has been 'lifted' from the Internet it must be a bit of a hit with others too.

PHOTOGRAPHIC EQUIPMENT USED

Nikon D300 DSLR, Micro Nikkor 70/180mm set on 180mm, f16, duration of synchronised flashes 1/1000s, ISO 200. Image was cropped by about 40 per cent in Photoshop CS5.

SPECIES

Northern Snapping Turtle (*Elseya dentata*)

PHOTOGRAPHER

Etienne Littlefair

STATUS

EX   EW   CR   EN   VU   NT   **LC**

LOCATION

Batchelor area, Northern Territory

NOTES

Average length around 30cm, with large head and thick shell. Herbivorous as adults and usually feed on ripening fruits that fall from trees overhanging the water.

STORY BEHIND THE PHOTO

This photo was taken on 12 July 2018 at 2pm. Members of the genus *Elseya* are referred to as snapping turtles, although in truth they are predominately herbivorous in their eating habits and I have never witnessed one attempt to bite – rather they tend to make themselves scarce when other large organisms such as humans enter their zone of comfort.

The Northern Snapping Turtle is prevalent across much of the western portion of the Top End, where I have seen them from Darwin region to as far south as Katherine and west to the Timber Creek area. The species tends to favour deep pools with rocky bottoms, lined at least partially with dense overhanging vegetation including *Pandanus* where the youngsters reside. Adults are most likely to be encountered in the open or by shining a light under large rocks – of course being mindful of other creatures that could inhabit these caves and crevices. I once followed a large specimen down to a crevice and as it entered a 1.5m Freshwater Crocodile emerged, much to my delight. In waterways with high numbers of Freshwater Crocodiles, this species and short-necked turtles from the genus *Emydura* are often short a limb or two – presumably from attempted predation – although this doesn't seem to hinder their movement much. Interestingly, I have rarely noticed missing limbs on long-necked turtles of the genus *Chelodina*, suggesting that they are perhaps somewhat better at avoiding predation than their cousins.

There are two things that stand out about this photo. One is that this is the largest specimen of *Elseya dentata* that I have encountered to date, close to the purported upper size dimension these turtles can achieve. The other is that this turtle was photographed in full sun in a deep pool around 8m below the surface, which is the reason for the delightful sunrays behind the specimen. Photographs that show something of the habitat of these denizens of the deep are difficult to achieve at best, especially for large adults, as they are typically most active under conditions of deep shade, following crepuscular activity patterns.

A final requisite is required to achieve views and photographs of this species – water clarity. Escarpment pools in the Top End are often referred to as 'crystal clear', but to a photographer and turtle watcher this is only true for a few short weeks preceding the end of the wet season when the turbidity from the final bout of heavy rain settles, having washed all the tannin and sediment from waterways. From May to mid-July it is possible to locate these turtles from the surface down to around 12m in certain areas, making this a freshwater snorkelling paradise.

PHOTOGRAPHIC EQUIPMENT USED

Olympus EM1 Mark II, Olympus 7–14mm f2.8 lens, Nauticam housing, Sea and Sea strobes. Processed using Adobe Photoshop CC.

SPECIES

Yellow-headed Snapping Turtle (*Elseya irwini*)

PHOTOGRAPHER

John Cann

STATUS

EX EW CR EN VU NT **LC**

LOCATION

Reported to have come from a tributary of the Burdekin River, north Queensland.

NOTES

One of our largest and most attractive turtle species. Carapace lengths of more than 33cm have been recorded. Once the species was formally described, it was named after Bob Irwin and his son Steve.

STORY BEHIND THE PHOTO

This specimen of was photographed in an aquarium at night in October 2013 using three flashes. It was one of possibly 20 images of this particular animal, and it also appears on the cover of my book *Freshwater Turtles of Australia*, which was published in 2017.

I had never seen a large male of this species until a friend rang and told me that a chap had just brought one to him. I made contact and was given this attractive turtle on loan to photograph.

This species, which is also known as Irwin's Snapping Turtle, is restricted to the Burdekin River drainage in northern Queensland. The Burdekin River is more than 2,000km from where I live, but I have been there on a number of occasions, this time to a location known as Broken River – one of the main tributaries starting high in the ranges via Eungella. The route to the river where I go to see *Elseya irwini* is through private property which is reasonably flat country, before dropping down to the river along several kilometres of a twisting bulldozed track. I must admit that I was quite concerned, not due to my driving ability, but because of potential brake failure on the steep bending descent. Once off the range the track is quite good and to the north downstream there is a nice flat grassed area where the homesteaders camp when working their cattle or line fishing.

At this point on the Broken River the depth is on average 1.5m, normally very clear, with a sandy bottom and in areas many boulders that these turtles often use for shelter. Also present in the river are the Saw-shelled Turtle (*Wollumbinia latisternum*) and Krefft's Turtle (*Emydura krefftii*), but these are only rarely seen. The location where the type specimen was collected is further downstream in Saltwater Crocodile county, and where large Bull sharks have been caught, so diving is not advised. Here in sandy patches are numbers of black water snails growing to 10mm, which the *Elseya irwini* eat in large quantities.

Some regard the snapping turtle from the Johnstone Rivers to the north as the same species based on information from early DNA, and although they seem to be closely related I believe they should at least be regarded as different subspecies, based on the significant differences in male colouration and hatchlings between the Burdekin and Johnstone River populations.

PHOTOGRAPHIC EQUIPMENT USED

Nikon D80, Nikon Macro lens and three flashes.

SPECIES

Mary River Turtle (*Elusor macrurus*)

PHOTOGRAPHER

Gary Stephenson

STATUS

EX   EW   CR   **EN**   VU   NT   LC

LOCATION

Mary River, Queensland

NOTES

A large and fascinating species with individuals of more than 50cm being recorded. The original 'Penny Turtle' with an estimated 150,000 sold in pet shops across Australia in the 1960s and 1970s. They are slow to mature, with females reaching sexual maturity at 25 years and males at 30.

STORY BEHIND THE PHOTO

My involvement with what was initially referred to as the 'Pet Shop Turtle' goes back to the 1960s pre-protection and when this species was readily available in pet shops across eastern Australia. The conundrum was: from where did this unique species originate and what did the adults look like, as it was only juveniles that were available in pet shops?

Cann and Sadlier's 2017 *Freshwater Turtles of Australia* gives a detailed account of locating in the wild what is now known as the Mary River Turtle. It is listed as an endangered species. Referenced in this book is an adult female I found in 1979 in Sydney, in one of Centennial Park's lakes, some 1,200km south of the Mary River. It is likely that this specimen was released into the lake as one of many unwanted pets.

Neither John Cann nor myself retained the measurements for the Centennial Park specimen but I remember it like it was yesterday, being a somewhat largish animal by comparison to then known similar species. When the first wild population was confirmed near Tiaro and further work was done establishing the large size this species reaches, the world of Australian 'short-necked turtles' changed forever because this is the only known species where males are larger than females.

The Mary River Turtle illustrated here is a large female – the longitudinal grooves in the carapace are testament to its advanced age.

Mary River Turtles can be observed basking on logs that had either fallen into or have been washed into the river by floods. When disturbed, these turtles will seek refuge amongst the fallen logs, which (along with the turbid water) presents its own challenges for divers attempting to observe this species in the wild. Large specimens such as this and the even bigger males are extremely fast swimmers, so to observe these turtles in their natural environment I use a good quality face mask, fins (for speed) and a snorkel. You need to be a better than average swimmer and be able to hold your breath for considerable periods.

It is pleasing to report that farmers along the Mary River are now fencing off known nesting beaches where in the past cattle would come down to drink and trample not only the Mary River Turtle nests, but also those of the critically endangered Southern Snapping Turtle (*Elseya albagula*). It is also this same livestock that in part causes the turbidity in the Mary River.

PHOTOGRAPHIC EQUIPMENT USED

Nikon D300s body with Nikkor 18–200mm 3.5 – 5.6 G ED zoom lens at 45mm, f14, 1/125s, ISO 200. Camera-mounted Nikon Speedlight SB-600 on manual setting at ¼ power and 4 'slave' flash guns mounted about 300mm above a large rectangular aquarium fitted out to replicate the Mary River. The master flash is at the same level but approximately 600mm in front of the glass, pointing towards the inside of tank. Processed in Photoshop CS2 with some image sharpening, removal of highlights and colour enhancement.

SPECIES

Clarence River Turtle (*Emydura macquarii binjing*)

PHOTOGRAPHER

John Cann

STATUS

EX EW CR EN VU NT **LC**

LOCATION

Clarence River, New South Wales

NOTES

A reasonably small species – average carapace length 20cm. First described by John Cann in 1998. Pronounced 'bin-jing', the name had been used by Aboriginal inhabitants of the Clarence River to refer to the turtle for generations. Still very little is known about the natural history of this species, although clutch sizes of up to 11 eggs have been recorded.

STORY BEHIND THE PHOTO

This photograph was taken in the 1990s in an aquarium with four flashlights. Although I've taken others since, this one, to me, tells the story of this wonderful turtle. The image is now over a quarter of a century old, and was scanned from the old slide film and brought it back to its original condition. I described this turtle as a subspecies of coastal *Emydura* in 1998. At that time I restricted it to the Clarence River drainage – one of the largest river systems on the coast of New South Wales, being 400km in length. This turtle was collected in the Clarence where it runs close by the Aboriginal settlement known as Baryulgil. On the occasions that I stayed there I was invited to live with the Walker family, and Derrick Walker took me to a water hole nearby where a large dead tree with many limbs in the water would provide some protection for the turtles.

Derrick said: "I will get you one."

"Hang on," was my reply, "I will put on my diving gear."

He just dived in – no gear, just with his shorts – and surfaced with four 'binjing' in his hands! It is something that will stay always in my now fading memory. Binjing is the name given to this turtle by the Bundjalung People, and the name of the town Baryulgil means 'The sleeping lizard'. The village was built near an asbestos mine, and I recall many years ago that there was the wrongly conceived idea of spreading the tailings for the youngsters to play in. There have been many articles and books written on that playground. Fortunately not all were affected – Tony Mundine and family lived just across from the covered track.

In my 1998 book *Australian Freshwater Turtles* I mentioned the vast numbers of freshwater *Emydura* taken for food throughout the different villages along the Clarence and its many long branches. Photos recently forwarded to me show many heading to the cooking plates and open fires, no doubt one of the cherished bush foods. The locals on this river have now been collecting turtles, eels, Murray cod, and Bass for many thousands of years. Let us hope that this can continue, but I have concerns that this will be the case given the advanced diving equipment, effective traps and illegal nets, and modern travel methods used. I feel that these issues, in combination with some known and unknown man-made factors, mean that these and other turtles throughout Australia are in trouble.

Derrick has now passed away. He became a JP and as a youth he looked like the boxer Cassius Clay. I had the honour of giving the bride away at his wedding.

PHOTOGRAPHIC EQUIPMENT USED

Nikkormat PX camera with flashes. Slide film scanned with a Nikon Coolscan 9000 ED.

SPECIES

Northern Yellow-faced Turtle (*Emydura tanybaraga*)

PHOTOGRAPHER

Etienne Littlefair

STATUS

EX   EW   CR   EN   VU   NT   **LC**

LOCATION

Katherine area, Northern Territory

NOTES

Large size variance between the sexes, with females growing to 28.5cm but males rarely exceeding 16.7cm. Adults herbivorous, feeding on aquatic vegetation and overhanging fruits.

STORY BEHIND THE PHOTO

This image was taken shortly before 9am on 27 December 2018. This interesting species can be difficult to distinguish from the closely related Worrell's Turtle (*Emydura subglobosa worrelli*) in the field where they occur in sympatry. In fact there is much debate between researchers about the species status of certain *Emydura* populations in far north Queensland. Whether witnessing the last moments of crepuscular activity or simply that turtles remain active in deeper, darker pools throughout the day, early morning before the sun is high and too much light filters through the overhanging creek banks and aquatic vegetation is generally a good time to be in the water if one hopes to see turtles. I have found that in warm Top End waters turtles largely disappear from mid-morning until late afternoon when the shadows grow long. I also find that turtles are far more approachable in deeper, darker water, possibly as it is harder for them to perceive humans as a threat.

The flip side to this is that accessing turtles at depth requires excellent free diving ability, lung capacity, and willpower to overcome the innate fear of deep water and its denizens, namely crocodiles. Saltwater Crocodiles can occur in almost any Top End water body, even in areas managed for public swimming. My wife Cara and I avoid 'Salties' by ensuring we have good, up to date local knowledge and have personally surveyed, day and night, any waters we plan to enter. We also use topography to our advantage, accessing waters above high waterfalls or small, shallow segments of creeks in between cascades and rapids.

To take this image I located a large overhanging bank of around 3m deep where a turtle would glide by every few minutes – an underwater reptile photographers dream. Once I was in position, I waited until a large turtle entered my field of view and simply sank slowly to the creek bed in the dark as the turtle approached me, visible only by its faint outline. It seemed aware of my presence as it approached and investigated me, but unlike when I encounter this species in the open water, here is showed no fear and simply carried on swimming, allowing me to capture this stunning, natural image. I would not have been able to take this image but for the amazing autofocus capabilities of the Nikon D850, which focused perfectly on the turtle's eye at f18. This technique has allowed me to capture many turtle images over the past two years that otherwise may not have been possible.

PHOTOGRAPHIC EQUIPMENT USED

Nikon D850 with Nikkor 8–15mm f3.5-4.5 lens, Nauticam housing, Sea and Sea strobes. Processed using Adobe Photoshop CC.

SPECIES

Northern Red-faced Turtle (*Emydura victoriae*)

PHOTOGRAPHER

Etienne Littlefair

STATUS

 EX EW CR EN VU NT **LC**

LOCATION

Manning River, The Kimberley, Western Australia

NOTES

Average size around 25cm. In 1997 six were removed from the wild for display at Perth Zoo. At the time little was known of their reproductive biology, but the zoo was able to breed eight clutches over a two-year period, with an average clutch size of 10 eggs.

STORY BEHIND THE PHOTO

Late afternoon is frequently a reliable time to see diurnal freshwater turtle activity in the tropical north of Australia. This photo was taken shortly before 4pm on 19 June 2018. I'd like to say that this shot was planned and perfectly executed, but it was in fact somewhat of a fluke; I had just put myself in the right place at the right time.

This young turtle had a total length of approximately 6–7cm and is pictured here swimming quickly along a creek bank after being disturbed. I've consistently found this species to be one of the hardest Australian turtles to photograph due to their shy nature and tendency to flee at incredible speeds once they're aware of my presence, but on this occasion I got lucky. The turtle decided to flee between my camera and the nearby bank, where usually they disappear into the *Pandanus* root system never to be seen again.

Generally, photographing young turtles in tropical Australia is challenging for a few key reasons: predation and recruitment declines. Young turtles face predation from crocodiles, large catfish, barramundi and water birds, and practice predator avoidance by remaining hidden in creek banks and occasionally under rocks; some species have very close ties with overhanging *Pandanus* plants in particular. Relating to this, fire regimes feature prominently in turtle habitat occupancy. Well-vegetated banks typically have turtles; areas that have been burnt, and lose overhanging vegetation, typically do not host turtles. Recruitment declines are partially attributed to feral pig populations; impacted waterways are often identifiable by evidence of trampling and even a faint farmyard smell; and pigs love to feast on turtle eggs. A factor becoming more prevalent in determining turtle recruitment is climate change – eggs need to be incubated within a specific temperature range in order to hatch successfully and for many species incubation temperature determines offspring sex. There is emerging evidence that recent hot years have had severe impacts on nesting success across various turtle populations, including those of the Gulf Snapping turtle (*Elseya lavarackorum*). In the future this may also lead to skewed sex ratios, further impacting recruitment potential. In many areas my wife and I snorkel it is exceedingly rare to glimpse young turtles, even when adult specimens may be relatively abundant; to date I have never seen a young long-necked turtle in the Top End. For these reasons I am overjoyed whenever I encounter a young turtle and find hope that these populations will persist into the future.

PHOTOGRAPHIC EQUIPMENT USED

Olympus EM1 Mark II, Olympus 7–14mm f2.8 lens, Nauticam housing, Sea and Sea strobes. Processed using Adobe Photoshop CC.

SPECIES

Fitzroy River Turtle (*Rheodytes leukops*)

PHOTOGRAPHER

John Cann

STATUS

EX EW CR EN **VU** NT LC

LOCATION

Fitzroy River, Queensland

NOTES

This unique turtle is the only surviving member of the genus *Rheodytes*. Both sexes average around 26cm. Unlike many other short-necked turtle species, a large part of the diet is made up of macroinvertebrates, as well as freshwater sponges, algae, aquatic snails and worms.

STORY BEHIND THE PHOTO

This photograph was taken at night, possibly with five flashlights, three on top of my 4x3ft. aquarium, and two on tripods. The two turtles in the image were collected in late September 1976 under John Legler's permit when he came to Australia from Utah University, USA, over a number of years collecting freshwater 'tortoises' as they were referred to prior to 1998. John had temporarily left Australia and authorised for me to do research for him (and myself) under his permits.

This species is only known from the Fitzroy River system. During the trip on which these turtles were collected, I had had set up camp near the river with my wife and our three youngsters in a large tent at a location known as Fitzroy Crossing, where there is raised concrete causeway. At this location the river was wide upstream, at least 100m, while downstream of the causeway it narrowed to a quite rocky stretch for a few hundred metres or more, then widened into a large oxbow-shaped pool around 400m wide. It was here that Legler and myself encountered a 2m Saltwater Crocodile several years earlier with our spotlights when we were setting drum nets from a dingy for turtles. My wife Helen remembered this incident well as we had spoken about it numerous times and she refused to enter the water at the narrow crossing, only at the outlets of the then working spillway.

At 'warm time' my sons – who were good swimmers at the ages of nine and ten, having dived with me on numerous occasions along the New South Wales coastal rivers – were with me bagging Fitzroy River Turtles along the narrow rocky, shallow section. As we came closer to the oxbow the water became murky, deeper and wider, and I suggested to the boys that 'this will do'. I did not have to repeat it, and they moved quickly close behind me, much to Helen's relief. It was just as well, because about 50m downstream at the opening of the oxbow was the largest croc that I have ever spotted, sinking down from the paperbark and other trees into the creepy glum. Measurements of the turtles caught were taken and all except this pair were released. The only turtles seen on this outing were Fitzroy River Turtles, although five other species of chelids occur in this massive river system.

PHOTOGRAPHIC EQUIPMENT USED

Nikon F108 camera with flashes. Canoscan 9000 F Mark II.

SPECIES

Bell's Turtle (*Wollumbinia belli*)

PHOTOGRAPHER

John Cann

STATUS

EX EW CR **EN** VU NT LC

LOCATION

Namoi River on the New South Wales northern tablelands

NOTES

Carapace length around 30cm for females and 22.7cm for males. Exhibits high incidence of eye disease – appearing as cloudiness or cataracts – affecting 14 per cent of adults in populations upstream, to more than 50 per cent in populations further downstream.

STORY BEHIND THE PHOTO

The turtle in this photograph was collected on the Namoi River in 2002. The species was first shown by me in my 1978 book *Tortoises of Australia*, where it was presented as an undescribed species of *Elseya*. However, it turned out that this turtle had been described more than a hundred years earlier as *Phrynops bellii* by John Gray of the British Museum in 1844, but had been overlooked by researchers, probably because no location data was given by the time of description that would associate it with Australian turtles. The existence of this specimen in the collection of the British Museum was first noted by well-known turtle researcher from the USA, Anders Rhodin, who sent me images of the preserved specimen in 1980. On seeing these photos I considered that it may be one of the turtles from the rivers of the New England Tableland, the 'undescribed' species from the Namoi and Gwydir River drainages I had referred to in my 1978 book.

I tried tracing some of the possible history of this specimen in the British Museum, and concluded it was likely obtained by the noted 19th century naturalist and collector John Gould. However, proving that it was Gould, or others who worked for or supplied various specimens of animals to Gray, was a long and difficult matter. The break finally came when I discovered that Gould had travelled as far as Tamworth collecting specimens, and that Gray had also described the Swamp Rat from a specimen supplied by Gould. Both animals had likely come from the McDonald River, where Gould's brother-in-law owned Bendameer homestead, 32km from Tamworth. The three rivers mentioned all link up, supporting the connection between the specimen and the collector. Later investigations using both morphology and genetics have supported my earlier conclusion as to the identity of the type specimen of *Phrynops bellii* – a different way of 'discovering' a species of turtle.

Today the numbers of *Wollumbinia belli* appear to be dropping, and current research is underway to try to rectify this, but it will be a long and hard road to success. The rivers where this species lives on the high-elevation tablelands are in granite country, and it is not found below the escarpment. The riverbeds are sandy, but also in places quite rocky, and at many locations covered with various different water plants. Willow trees, paperbark and gums are common on the banks, but over-cleared in many locations. Windblown leaves of gum trees are often eaten by Bell's Turtles.

PHOTOGRAPHIC EQUIPMENT USED

Nikkormat PX camera with flashes. Slide film scanned on a Canon scanner.

SPECIES

Saw-shelled Turtle (*Wollumbinia latisternum*)

PHOTOGRAPHER

John Cann

STATUS

EX   EW   CR   EN   VU   NT   **LC**

LOCATION

Tweed River, New South Wales

NOTES

Reaches lengths of around 24cm. Has a serrated hind edge to the shell and distinctive spines on the neck. Predominantly carnivorous, they have been observed successfully preying on Cane Toads and appear immune to their poison, which is normally fatal when ingested.

STORY BEHIND THE PHOTO

This image was taken on Wednesday 13 November 2002. The algae on top of the head develops, then the water slows or stops flowing, possibly cools seasonally and the turtles rest until conditions are better for activity.

This individual is from the Tweed River and was caught at Byrrill Creek, just west of Kunghur in far north-east New South Wales. It was not my first visit to the Tweed River, and on this outing I drove from Sydney to Murwillumbah. As we had no set location to search we just 'played it by ear' as the saying goes. Any person who drives this river country will see the splendid sight of Mount Warning, the remnant of an ancient volcano, rising high above the surrounding countryside. Named by Captain Cook back in 1770 when his ship was almost grounded at what is now known as Danger Point, this mountain was already named by the Aboriginal nation, the Bundjalung People, as Wollumbin.

The Tweed runs for 160km to the sea, with its headwaters in a World Heritage-listed national park. Here the Saw-shelled Turtle lives together with one of the coastal *Emydura*, while the Broad-shelled Long-necked Turtle (*Chelodina expansa*) occurs in the coastal swamps and lagoons. The Tweed River varies greatly, like many mountain-to-sea rivers do, having a sandy bottom with rocky boulders, and large stretches of edible plants which are great food for short-necked turtles.

The generic name for the Australian saw-shelled turtles, *Wollumbinia*, was created by Richard Wells and refers to the Aboriginal name for Mount Warning. For a number of reasons this name has been declared invalid and rejected by a number of turtle workers, but has been accepted by others, including Dr Harold Cogger, who was a commissioner on the Board of Zoological Nomenclature for many years. I have my own thoughts, but I would prefer other decisions than mine.

PHOTOGRAPHIC EQUIPMENT USED

Nikon D80 with macro lens. No flash. Slide Film. Rescanned.

SPECIES

Chameleon Gecko (*Carphodactylus laevis*)

PHOTOGRAPHER

Michael Cermak

STATUS

EX   EW   CR   EN   VU   NT   **LC**

LOCATION

Mount Lewis, North Queensland

NOTES

Snout-vent length 13cm. A large species with a total length of 27cm. Like all geckos they lay two eggs at a time, with up to six clutches being laid in a season.

STORY BEHIND THE PHOTO

A tropical rainforest dweller admired by every herper and photographer. This species is mainly found in upland habitats but there are few lowland populations north of Cardwell. I photographed this particular individual at 860m above sea-level on Mount Lewis – my favourite herping grounds. On some nights I haven't come across any, but on a good night it's not unusual to find up to five of these cryptic geckos. They blend in well with their surroundings, so the best way to spot one is with a head torch.

Chameleon Geckos have the habit of tilting their heads downwards when hit with the light, effectively cancelling the eye-reflection. This makes them hard to find, especially when they are in the distance. That was the case when I spotted this one. The lights (its eye reflection) went out, so I stumbled through the undergrowth in roughly the right direction but soon realised that I was either too far or off to the side. I started walking in circles, wider and wider until I was completely lost as to where I first saw the gecko.

I made it back onto the track and scanned the ground again and again with the light and there it was. This time I was more familiar with the surroundings, so stepped out fast towards the animal but lost the eye-shine again when I was about 2m away. After a quick search I found my gecko. As often happens, the backdrop was awful for photography, but there was a nice mossy log only about a metre away – a perfect set up.

These geckos don't like to be handled, and they often drop their tail when treated roughly. I encouraged it to walk onto a stick and then off the stick onto the 'stage'. The plan went very smoothly and I was ready to shoot. Some 15 shots later I just walked away, leaving the beautiful creature to find his way home.

PHOTOGRAPHIC EQUIPMENT USED

Canon 1Ds Mark III, Canon 24–70mm L 2.8 lens, two Canon Speedlite EX600EX-RT flashguns, f16, 1/60s, ISO 100.

SPECIES

Centralian Knob-tailed Gecko (*Nephrurus amyae*)

PHOTOGRAPHER

Peter Soltys

STATUS

EX   EW   CR   EN   VU   NT   **LC**

LOCATION

Alice Springs, Northern Territory

NOTES

Snout-vent length 14cm. Not particularly productive, rarely laying more than two clutches per season, compared to other knob-tailed geckos, which have been recorded producing as many as nine clutches each year.

STORY BEHIND THE PHOTO

Every year around Christmas I like to go away for a few days, as Sydney has too many people around at that time. In December 2015 the plan was to visit Alice Springs. Not the best time of the year as it is way too hot in that area, however this place had been on my list for a long time, so I wanted to give it a go.

After arriving in Alice Springs, I picked up my rental car and started road cruising right away. As I usually do after a few hours of driving, I took a walk to refresh my mind in order to stay more focused. Exploring small outcrops along the road is a great way to search for knob-tailed geckos as this happens to be their habitat. It was around 1am. As knob-tailed geckos have very funny looking tails, I wanted to see these creatures badly, but did not have much luck. At this point, I had not seen any of the nine species so I set my mind to find one on this trip.

The night was fruitful: I saw a few Western Brown Snakes (*Pseudonaja mengdeni*), about six Desert Death Adders (*Acanthopis pyrrhus*) and a bunch of other geckos, but still no sign of a knob-tailed gecko. It was getting late, or to be more specific the early hours of the morning were ticking by, so after six hours of road cruising I decided to give up and get some rest.

Just as I turned the car around, I noticed a funny little thing sitting on the side of the road. Well well well – a knob-tailed gecko was about to cross the road. It was more mesmerising than I was expecting. Super-sharp spikes and that funny tail. So cool. By the time I reached the camp I saw another three. It was a great night. That night I saw about 14 new species for me, and this one was one of my favourites.

PHOTOGRAPHIC EQUIPMENT USED

Canon EOS 5D Mark III, Canon EF 24mm f1.4 Mark II USM, Canon Speedlight 600EX, combination of softbox and second diffusion, f18, 1/200s, ISO 100. Flash Setting – ETTL. Editing program – Lightroom Classic.

SPECIES

Prickly Knob-tailed Gecko (*Nephrurus asper*)

PHOTOGRAPHER

Gary Stephenson

STATUS

EX EW CR EN VU NT **LC**

LOCATION

Anakie, Queensland

NOTES

Snout-vent length 11.5cm. Heavy bodied with one individual weighing 61g. It is believed that all knob-tailed gecko species have a life expectancy of more than 20 years.

STORY BEHIND THE PHOTO

Exploring herping locations in northern Australia during the hotter and wetter months of the year is often done at night, because during the day not much reptile activity can be observed except for perhaps dragons and monitor lizards which may take flight at an approaching vehicle.

In hot and humid conditions some species generally considered to be diurnal will come to the road for warmth as the night air cools the atmosphere, and they also take the opportunity to search for 'roadkill' as an easy food source. In some diurnal species, particularly dragons, it's not uncommon to find these asleep and very much alive on the less travelled sealed roads.

In Australia, geckos are a common sight on our roads at night. With more than 70 species, this group of lizards is well represented in all mainland Australian states and territories and found in almost all environments.

The species in the family Carphodactylidae, such as this Prickly Knob-tailed Gecko, have a reputation for putting on an impressive defensive display when disturbed. This large specimen was located just after dusk on the Capricorn Highway near Anakie in central Queensland, and it was searching for insects to eat. As the Capricorn Highway is well travelled, particularly by heavy trucks, we relocated this specimen to an adjacent rock outcrop where almost on cue it put on this threat display – the only thing missing was the gaping mouth!

Knob-tailed geckos in the genus *Nephrurus* are either found in rocky or sandy (dune) environments. The exact purpose of the 'knob' tail is not known, but perhaps could be used as a plug to block access to burrows by predators. In any event, the tail comes in many shapes and sizes depending on the species, with Centralian (*N. amyae*), Prickly (*N. asper*) and Northern (*N. sheai*) having the smallest.

Also on the road that evening were Burton's Snake-lizards (*Lialis burtonis*), Black-headed Pythons (*Aspidites melanocephalus*), Stimson's Pythons (*Antaresia stimsoni*) and Mulga or King Brown Snakes (*Pseudechis australis*). All are potential predators of the Rough Knob-tailed Gecko, so it was not just the traffic that needed to be avoided!

PHOTOGRAPHIC EQUIPMENT USED

Nikon D50, Nikkor 105mm 1:2.8 D micro (prime) lens, f11, 1/125 sec, ISO 100. Camera-mounted Nikon Speedlight SB-600 on manual setting at ¼ power. Processed in Photoshop CS2 with some image sharpening, softening of shadows and minor adjustments to the white balance and colour.

SPECIES

Southern Banded Knob-tailed Gecko (*Nephrurus wheeleri wheeleri*)

PHOTOGRAPHER

Gunther Schmida

STATUS

EX   EW   CR   EN   VU   NT   **LC**

LOCATION

Studio, Gold Coast, Queensland

NOTES

Snout-vent length 10cm. Voracious feeder, like all knob-tailed geckos. Known to eat virtually anything they can overpower including spiders, cockroaches, crickets, scorpions, caterpillars, beetles, and even smaller geckos and skinks. Females generally lay three to five clutches per season, with two eggs per clutch.

STORY BEHIND THE PHOTO

I love geckos (actually all reptiles and more) but there is something special about knob-tailed geckos. I have photographed most of them in the wild and some in captive collections. As long as I can find the right backdrop, and shots don't look staged, I do not have a problem with it.

The Southern Banded Knob-tailed Gecko is one of my favourites, but sadly I cannot claim to have ever found one alive in its habitat in the Goldfields region of Western Australia, although I have been there, and seen road-kills. A bit of luck is always needed to encounter any reptile in nature, especially nocturnal ones.

Luckily, this gecko is also a favourite of many reptile keepers, and has been available in the hobby for some time now. The portrait of this subadult captive-bred specimen was photographed in my 'man cave' (studio) courtesy of Robert Porter, who has been breeding all manner of reptiles for many years and often supported me in my endeavours. Thanks Rob.

As all Australian geckos are nocturnal creatures I always use flash when taking photographs: usually two units, one as the main flash mounted on the camera shoe and another smaller one, attached with a bracket, as the fill-in to lighten the shadows. My home-made bracket also features a small LED torch for focusing purposes, when photographing in the wild in the dark of the night. Sometimes I use a soft-box on the main flash. Whatever gives me the result I am looking for. The fact that digital cameras allow us to check the lighting of all shots on their playback screen is greatly appreciated in a situation like this.

PHOTOGRAPHIC EQUIPMENT USED

Nikon D300 DSLR, Micro Nikkor 70/180mm set on180mm, f16, ISO 200. The image was cropped by about 20 per cent in Photoshop CS5.

SPECIES

Northern Leaf-tailed Gecko (*Saltuarius cornutus*)

PHOTOGRAPHER

Scott Eipper

STATUS

EX EW CR EN VU NT **LC**

LOCATION

Lake Barrine, Queensland

NOTES

Snout-vent length 14.5cm. Like all members of the leaf-tailed gecko group they have a spectacular threat display that involves arching the back and raising and wagging the tail from side to side in an attempt to draw attention away from the head, all while making a loud squealing noise.

STORY BEHIND THE PHOTO

This is one of Australia's largest geckos. Many people have successfully captured the amazing camouflage this and other species leaf-tailed geckos. In this image I planned to show a completely different side of their behaviour. Leaf-tailed geckos are ambush predators, spending hours sitting face-down on trees, vines and boulders awaiting various invertebrate prey.

I had determined my camera settings by experimenting with a water bottle on a stump, before attempting to find a gecko. I walked around in the rainforest at night carefully searching for the characteristic orange-red eye-shine. My camera was already set up when I found a lovely gecko with a perfect tail sitting about 80cm above the forest floor. I slowly inched forward with my light covered so as to not disturb the gecko. All was going to plan until my leg brushed against a small stinging tree. My leg burned intensely while I put down the camera and reached for the gaffer tape in my bag. I applied and reapplied the tape to remove the toxic hairs and get some relief. In all the commotion the gecko was now long gone. Disheartened and sore I started walking back towards the car when I spotted another individual – this time with a regenerated tail. Learning from my earlier experience, I checked the forest floor before positioning myself. The gecko sat in-situ for two images before deciding the other side of the tree was a better option for hunting. With my very sore leg I gave up, happy with an image that achieved what I was hoping for.

PHOTOGRAPHIC EQUIPMENT USED

Nikon D300, Nikkor 18–77 mm telephoto, three Nikon SB800 flashes (one camera mounted, two mounted to a Manfrotto twin flash bracket), f22, 1/250s, ISO 800, +.7 exposure bias.

SPECIES

Pretty Gecko (*Diplodactylus pulcher*)

PHOTOGRAPHER

Steve Swanson

STATUS

EX   EW   CR   EN   VU   NT   **LC**

LOCATION

Yalgoo, Western Australia

NOTES

Snout-vent length 5.5cm. Alternative name Fine-faced Gecko. Diet seems to consist exclusively of termites. Females lay one or two eggs in each reproductive cycle.

STORY BEHIND THE PHOTO

The Pretty Gecko is widespread in much of arid Western Australia. The Latin name *pulcher* means 'beautiful', and it certainly lives up to its name. Two distinct morphs are apparent: a 'blotched' morph and a 'striped' morph. I had a long-held ambition to find both morphs and photograph them together.

On a warm night in March 2015, a friend and I were spotlighting on a sandy plain near Yalgoo, Western Australia. The first reptile we encountered was a Monk Snake *(Parasuta monarchus)*, a species I was keen to photograph.

Over the next few hours we came across a number of Midline Knob-tailed Geckos *(Nephrurus vertebralis)*, Western-shield Spiny-tailed Geckos *(Strophurus wellingtonae)* and, eventually, both morphs of the Pretty Gecko.

PHOTOGRAPHIC EQUIPMENT USED

Pentax K10D, Pentax 90mm macro, f27, flash sync speed 1/180s. External flashgun mounted on camera hotshoe. Some minor adjustments to the image using Photoshop.

SPECIES

Duvaucel's Gecko (*Hoplodactylus duvauceli*)

PHOTOGRAPHER

Tony Jewell

STATUS

EX EW CR EN VU **NT** LC

LOCATION

Cromwell, Central Otago, South Island

NOTES

Snout-vent length 16cm. Nocturnal. Seems to reproduce once every two years, with an average litter size of two. Scientists have estimated that individuals can live for up to 50 years in the wild.

STORY BEHIND THE PHOTO

Mystery surrounds the extinct gecko fauna of New Zealand, with several early Maori accounts and long-lost bone relics hinting at the possible occurrence of giant species on both main islands. But a dearth of verifiable scientific evidence casts some doubt over this. The genus *Hoplodactylus* contains the two largest gecko species associated with New Zealand. *H. delcourti*, the world's largest gecko, is known from a single stuffed specimen of unknown origin. It has strong physical similarities with the New Zealand geckos, but also a few notable differences, and its placement in *Hoplodactylus* is at best tentative. We can speculate that it could just as easily have arisen in isolation from the New Zealand lineage, perhaps having split away from a common ancestor after becoming isolated in another island group. Wherever it came from, *H. delcourti* is almost certainly now extinct.

The other member of the genus, *H. duvauceli*, is in comparison lucky enough to count itself among the living. Subfossil bone remains suggest that it was once distributed across most of New Zealand, but the introduction of rats and other predators almost eliminated it. It survived on a handful of small offshore islands which escaped the rodent advance. At about 30cm in length it is only half the length of *H. delcourti*, but is still New Zealand's largest verified lizard species. Subfossil remains suggest that *H. duvauceli* once ranged at least as far south as Otago, in the southern South Island, which means that it would once have been a key player in the ecology of this region. Yet the climate and habitats of Otago differ significantly from anywhere that the species survives today.

When the opportunity arose to photograph some captive *H. duvauceli* in Otago it seemed like a great chance to portray the species as it may have looked in local environments. I had three specimens on loan for a few days and took all manner of images of one or two specimens among lichen-encrusted schist rocks surrounded by native drylands vegetation. While doing so I also took a few shots in other, less characteristic habitats, including this one of a specimen in a cabbage tree – a plant species common throughout New Zealand. The main challenge had been that my camera at the time, the Canon A80, had little capacity to focus in dim light, while the geckos themselves had equally little tolerance for bright light. In the end the inflexible limitations of the camera won over and the geckos had to endure the glaring Otago sunlight. This particular shot was taken in broad daylight at the entrance of my dry dusty driveway, with a cherry orchard, a busy road and a peacock not too far out of frame. Sometimes a good image depends as much on what can be framed out of the picture as what gets set up within it. This simple image of a gecko at the side of a dusty road ended up being far more satisfying than any of the shots I took among complex natural Otago surroundings.

PHOTOGRAPHIC EQUIPMENT USED

Canon A80 camera with an automated setting (f5.6, 1/25s, ISO 50) with auto focus and natural lighting. Image edited slightly with an exposure gradient over some foreground leaves to remove some excess glare.

SPECIES

Coromandel Striped Gecko (*Toropuku* 'Coromandel')

PHOTOGRAPHER

Dylan van Winkel

STATUS

EX EW CR **EN** VU NT LC

LOCATION

Coromandel Peninsula, Waikato, North Island

NOTES

Snout-vent length 8cm. Feeds on insects, fruit and nectar. Thought to live for more than 16 years. Unlike all other geckos found across the world, those from New Zealand give birth to live young – an adaptation due to the cold climate. They also produce fewer offspring, making all species at greater risk of extinction.

STORY BEHIND THE PHOTO

A gecko so elusive that it remained undetected for decades despite active survey and research interest across its range. It was first reported in 1997, after one was found clinging to the interior wall of a private residence in a small town. Its uncanny resemblance to the Striped Gecko (*Toropuku stephensi*) from South Island's Marlborough Sounds – 500km to the south – and the failure to find additional specimens meant there was lingering scepticism that the 1997 specimen represented a genuine and highly significant range extension.

It wasn't until two years later that another turned up – opportunistically discovered crossing a road – but still intensive searches in the vicinity could not locate additional individuals. It was nearly a decade before the next one was found, and attempts to radio track this individual to gain an understanding of its ecology failed as the gecko routinely found ways to escape from the transmitter harness. A public advocacy campaign resulted in a few more individuals being found in subsequent years, some of which were captured and assigned to a captive-breeding scheme. Genetic work confirmed that this was indeed a distinct taxon.

My most memorable encounter with this elusive critter came in late 2017, while preparing a new field guide to the New Zealand herpetofauna. I got wind that a community group had been sighting geckos on a large tract of predator-controlled bush in the Coromandel, so one night I headed to the site with James Reardon and Rhys Burns. We joined a small group of locals and began spotlighting through the dense forest and tangled vineland. Hours passed with only spiders and bugs to show for our efforts. Apparently a gecko had been seen in the area the night before, so we continued looking.

Just before midnight James sighted a gecko, but it disappeared into dense ferns. Within seconds three of us were attempting to resight the animal using our headlights. Reaching deep within the base of the fern, a small velvety body brushed past my hand. I caught a glimpse and lunged forward to grasp the gecko. We all gathered round as I slowly unravelled my fingers. There it was, arguably New Zealand's most elusive gecko. Its slender body and grasping hands reminded me of the spinifex-dwelling *Strophurus*; however, its hand morphology was markedly different, having distinctive webbing between the fingers and toes. Gasps were interrupted by James' words: "That's not the individual I saw". There must have been more than one in the fern! Perhaps unsurprising given the cryptic nature of these geckos. We collected morphological information, took some photographs and then released the gecko back into its lair. This image represents a traditional portrait of this rare and poorly known taxon.

PHOTOGRAPHIC EQUIPMENT USED

Canon 450D, Canon EF 100mm f/2.8 Macro USM Lens, 430EX II Speedlite with DIY diffuser. Adobe Photoshop Lightroom CC.

SPECIES

Lister's Gecko (*Lepidodactylus listeri*)

PHOTOGRAPHER

Hal Cogger

STATUS

EX **EW** CR EN VU NT LC

LOCATION

Murray Hill area, Christmas Island, Indian Ocean

NOTES

Snout-vent length 5cm. Opportunistic hunter feeding on a broad spectrum of small invertebrates, with termites, small beetles, bugs and slaters forming the majority of their diet. Breeding occurs year-round, and clutches consist of two eggs and have been found under bark of trees.

STORY BEHIND THE PHOTO

In April 1979, Ross Sadlier and I had been searching for this endemic species for several nights in the rainforest on the central plateau of Christmas Island National Park without success. It's a species endemic to Christmas Island, and the world's specialist on the genus at that time – Walter Brown – while recognising this species, had been unable to find any distinguishing morphological features between it and its congener *Lepidodactylus manni*, which is found only in far-off Fiji.

Late in the night we were examining a number of tall rainforest trees standing naked in the middle of a bare phosphate minefield – they had been left as nesting trees for the threatened Abbott's Booby. On the lower trunk we found a female Lister's Gecko, then some nearby eggs under the loose bark at the tree's base. So this individual was photographed on the spot in case no others were found.

As it turned out, the species proved common and was found through a wide range of island habitats. However on a return survey in 1998, although we found a few specimens, they were much less abundant – or maybe just harder to find – than in 1979. But in the two decades between our visits Christmas Island's ecology was devastatingly impacted by the formation of supercolonies of the invasive Yellow Crazy Ant (*Anoplolepis gracilipes*). Introduced many years earlier without serious impact on the island's vertebrates, the ant had started to form supercolonies, each covering an area of up to several hectares, in which any animal passing through a colony's area would be overwhelmed by a mass attack of biting ants.

This had a devastating effect on the islands plants and animals, reducing the numbers of the island's famous land crabs and leading to the development of dense forest undergrowth in the absence of scavenging crabs. Most lizards had to abandon areas occupied by the crazy ant. The introduction of the Oriental Wolf Snake to Christmas Island in the mid-1980s put additional pressure on this gecko.

The last Lister's Gecko seen in the wild was in 2008, by which time a number of individuals had been taken into captivity by Christmas Island National Park's staff, where they formed the foundation stock of two large captive-breeding programs – one at Taronga Zoo in Sydney and the other on Christmas Island. The captive-breeding programs have so far produced more than 2,000 geckos that are to be used in attempts to reintroduce the species into the wild. For the time being it is formally classified as 'extinct in the wild'.

PHOTOGRAPHIC EQUIPMENT USED

Leica 1G camera with attached mirror reflex housing and 65mm macro Leitz Elmar lens on 100 ASA Kodachrome film and using low-output flashes. Age and projection dust and scratches were removed in Photoshop CS6 after scanning.

SPECIES

Yellow-snouted Ground Gecko (*Lucasium occultum*)

PHOTOGRAPHER

Chris Jolly

STATUS

EX   EW   CR   **EN**   VU   NT   LC

LOCATION

Point Stuart, Northern Territory

NOTES

Snout-vent length 4cm. Only 10 individual Yellow-snouted Geckos have ever been reported, from a total of about 22,000 trap-nights carried out across their range. In 2000 a wild-caught pair were brought into captivity at the Territory Wildlife Park, where they produced 12 hatchlings in a 12-month period.

STORY BEHIND THE PHOTO

This photo was taken in November 2017. The Yellow-snouted Ground Gecko is listed as endangered in the Northern Territory. Between its description in 1982 and its threatened species assessment in 2012, only 10 individuals had been found and officially recorded.

Despite seeming to be exceptionally rare in the wild, in actual fact they appear to be quite common in the right habitat. However, they only occur in a very particular habitat type, in a very restricted area.

These geckos are restricted to gravelly soils in the Wildman River region, between the Mary River to the west, the South Alligator River to the east and the Stuart Highway to the south.

Unfortunately, despite being rightfully listed as threatened, nothing has been done to truly assess the status of this species in the wild, nor has there been a recovery plan enacted. In fact, we currently have no knowledge of even its most basic ecology.

PHOTOGRAPHIC EQUIPMENT USED

Canon 7D, Canon 60mm macro, Canon 430EX II twin speedlites and Adobe Lightroom.

SPECIES

Forest Gecko (*Mokopirirakau granulatus*)

PHOTOGRAPHER

Dylan van Winkel

STATUS

EX EW CR EN **VU** NT LC

LOCATION

West Coast, South Island

NOTES

Snout-vent length 9cm. Another long-lived gecko, with captive animals having a life expectancy of 20–30 years. A nocturnal, arboreal species that gives birth to two live young in summer. Known to feed on insects, fruit and nectar.

STORY BEHIND THE PHOTO

There is a place in New Zealand where invertebrates are giants, plants are dwarfs, birds flightless and the lizards… well, they are spectacular! This is the result of millions of years of evolution, culminating in a unique but sensitive ecosystem which our generation is now responsible for protecting. It's a real pity that this place lies on top of a rich coal seam and is thus under threat of destruction.

Following intense media coverage and public outcries against planned mining operations, several photos emerged showcasing the site's wondrous lizard fauna. My mind blown, I had to visit. In early 2016 I arrived at the site and the immense area of seemingly suitable lizard habitat was overwhelming. However, for those familiar with herping in New Zealand, good habitat doesn't correlate with high lizard abundance. Our herpetofauna has suffered severe range contractions and declines in abundance as a result of exotic predatory mammals that have learned to exploit the naive, protein-rich packages that come in the form of our indigenous lizards. So, standing there looking over the site and with only an hour of daylight remaining, I knew I was in for a challenge. I looked at my camera thinking 'what's the point', before tucking it under the car seat and heading off across the weathered sandstone.

If you are familiar with the cartoon character 'Taz', you may understand my approach to herping this challenging environment under time pressure. Moving at superhuman speeds, in a spinning vortex across the landscape, searching vegetation, torch-lighting crevices, clambering up sandstone scarps, and turning rocks (carefully replacing them, of course) to reveal anything reminiscent of a lizard. My efforts were fruitless and with 20 minutes of daylight left I gave up.

I found an easier route back across large flat rock slabs. Disappointed, my mind turned to how and when I would next get back here to try my luck. Then I snapped out of this defeated mindset and a big sandstone slab caught my eye. I slowly turned it over. There, compressed against the ground, was a gecko unlike any I had ever seen before. Its background colour was grey overlaid with irregular patches of mahogany and burgundy, mirroring the colour of the surrounding rocks and the reddish lichen that decorated them. Even its eyes resembled the surrounding landform, with a darkened network of fine markings, overlaid with orange and red patches. It was one of the most outrageous examples of *Mokopirirakau granulatus* I had ever seen. I slowly lowered the rock back over the gecko and 'Usain Bolt'ed' it back to the car to retrieve my camera. Fortunately the gecko was still there when I returned, and in the faded light I repositioned it on a rock and fired off a few shots.

This image demonstrates the gecko's excellent camouflage. By flattening itself, masking its body contour, and mimicking the pattern of the local environment, it merges into its surroundings.

PHOTOGRAPHIC EQUIPMENT USED

Canon 450D, Canon EF 100mm f/2.8 Macro USM Lens, 430EX II Speedlite with DIY diffuser. Adobe Photoshop Lightroom CC.

SPECIES

Black-eyed Gecko (*Mokopirirakau kahutarae*)

PHOTOGRAPHER

Dylan van Winkel

STATUS

EX EW CR EN **VU** NT LC

LOCATION

Kahurangi National Park, Nelson Region, South Island

NOTES

Snout-vent length 9cm. Estimated life expectancy for captive animals is 20–30 years. Even by New Zealand standards this species is a cold-weather specialist, living in alpine zones up to 2,200m and recorded foraging in air temperatures as low as 6°C.

STORY BEHIND THE PHOTO

One of New Zealand's many unique and wonderful reptile species has always piqued my interest. It was described in 1984 by one of my heroes, the legendary Tony Whitaker, from the mountains in eastern Marlborough. This gecko is truly an alpine inhabitant, occurring at altitudes up to 2,200m, in environments that are completely covered in snow for at least three months of the year. Its yellow lips and huge jet-black eyes instantly distinguish it from all other geckos known from New Zealand.

The species I am referring to is the Black-eyed Gecko. It is best known from the Seaward Kaikoura Ranges, but a second population was discovered in 1998 approximately 120km to the west, in the Kahurangi National Park, by Tony and colleagues. Since this time, no dedicated follow-up searches had been undertaken at the site. I was intrigued. Did the species still persist there? This was enough inspiration for me to visit in December 2016, but days of searching proved fruitless.

Three months later I returned with two colleagues and we hiked for hours before establishing camp close to the ridgeline. We dedicated the afternoon to exploring the cliffs and finding safe routes to walk later that night while spotlighting. The mountains in this area have impressive exposed marble outcrops and vertical cliff faces heavily fissured with crevices extending for metres into the sides of the mountains, which is where the geckos take refuge from low winter temperatures.

That night we searched the marble faces with torches and binoculars, clinging to the vertical rocks with only the light from our headlights to guide the placement of our feet and hands. At about 3am, a gecko's reflective eyes appeared in my torchlight. I approached slowly but suddenly it was gone, and we could not relocate it. Disappointed, we headed back to camp only to find that a Weka had broken into my tent and helped itself to all my snacks. Not only that – the food had obviously not agreed with the bird's stomach. Say no more.

On our final day in the mountains I spent hours searching screes at the bottom of the cliffs and morale could not have been any lower. Sitting on a boulder taking a drink of water, I lazily flipped a rock beside me and the tip of a grey tail disappeared under one of the smaller boulders beneath. I jumped up and carefully lifted rock by rock until, finally, my fingers got hold of a small torso. I had him… a Black-eyed Gecko. This was the first one captured on the mountain for almost 20 years. Ecstatic, we all gathered to examine the animal – an adult male with a relatively short tail, orange lips, orange soles to the feet and huge black eyes. It was late afternoon, so I placed the animal on a boulder and positioned the camera to capture it in the foreground with the dramatic mountains behind. As the sun set, the sky had an orange glow. This fitting photograph portrays the gecko in its dramatic environment and provides a subtle hint about its nocturnal habits.

PHOTOGRAPHIC EQUIPMENT USED

Canon 450D, Venus Laowa 15mm f/4 1:1 Wide Angle Macro, 430EX II Speedlite with DIY diffuser, Adobe Photoshop Lightroom CC.

SPECIES

Tautuku Gecko (*Mokopirirakau* sp.)

PHOTOGRAPHER

Tony Jewell

STATUS

EX   EW   CR   **EN**   VU   NT   LC

LOCATION

Maclennan Range in the Catlins District, South Island

NOTES

Snout-vent length 8.5cm. Estimated life expectancy 20–30 years in captivity. Females give birth to one or two live young during summer.

STORY BEHIND THE PHOTO

When I was growing up in southern New Zealand in the 1980s, the local Forest Geckos were little more than a myth. My local museum at Riverton had an old jar filled with preserving fluid in which several faded old 19th-century lizard specimens were displayed, including two local examples of this supposedly common and widespread species. But no matter how carefully I searched the forests and shrublands around Riverton I just could not detect them. Indeed, when I approached some of our top herpetologists, they were as stumped as I was about why these geckos were seemingly impossible to detect in the far south. They were also suspicious that these very isolated populations may represent a distinct new species, but a lack of material suitable for study kept this idea firmly in the realm of a hunch. The last known records, I was told, were from the nearby Catlins district, where the geckos were rumoured to be especially beautifully coloured, including some with striking blue eyes.

On my first visit to the Catlins in 1994 I sighted a 'Forest Gecko', and based on this progress the Department of Conservation sent a small team to try and procure a specimen so that its identity could be resolved. We captured the one I had seen, and found another at a nearby site, and the study of these representatives confirmed them as an entirely separate species which is today known as Tautuku Gecko.

It was to be another ten years before a third specimen was located. Clearly very rare and difficult to detect, the species retains a near-mythical status. Shown here is one of a now growing number of individuals to have been seen in the podocarp rainforests of the Catlins, where they live on the trunks of great old rimu trees and among manuka (tea tree) along the sunny margins of clearings.

My objective was to find a way to illustrate the blue iris for which the species is known, but which is in reality quite fickle and in many individuals entirely absent. The gecko was found beneath a piece of wood and placed on a nearby tree where the moss closely matched its colouration. The blue in the eye was quite weak when viewed side-on, but front-on it stood out more clearly. To further bring out the blue, I aimed for a neutral black background. So I approached the gecko with the camera from the front and from below, so that the eyes were set against the backdrop rather than the tree, and the use of a flash light and a distant dull background ensured the background came out black. This angle also had the advantage of projecting most of the shadowing cast by the flash harmlessly into the black background beyond.

With few people ever getting to see rare species like this, I have found photography to be a critical tool for both education and conservation, providing a window into an otherwise completely hidden world. And when the subject emits charisma like this gecko does, it provides an invaluable emotional connection that helps get more people interested and involved in their study.

PHOTOGRAPHIC EQUIPMENT USED

Canon 400D, 900 mm Tamron macro lens, a medium f-stop (f16) to help darken the background, a low ISO (100) to keep the colours rich, and a shutter speed of 1/100s with the pop-up flash on.

SPECIES

Elegant Gecko (*Naultinus elegans*)

PHOTOGRAPHER

Dylan van Winkel

STATUS

EX   EW   CR   EN   *VU*   NT   LC

LOCATION

Auckland Region, North Island

NOTES

Snout-vent length 7cm. Alternative name Auckland Green Gecko. Unlike most of the world's geckos they are arboreal and diurnal. Like all New Zealand geckos they give birth to live young and have been reported to have gestation periods of up to a year. Estimated to live for 25 years in captivity.

STORY BEHIND THE PHOTO

It was 6.30pm on 27 April 2017 when I loaded my gear into the car and took off down the motorway heading north from Auckland. I had a big night ahead of me, the iced coffee and chocolate bar necessities for keeping focussed and maintaining maximum excitement. An hour and half later I arrived at my destination to greet the small group of equally excited 'gecko frothers'. We piled into the 4x4 MULE and headed up the hill, dodging rabbits in our headlights and veering around the odd sheep or twelve. We were on our way to a discrete area of parkland to commence our annual gecko-monitoring survey work for the local council.

We arrived at the start of the track just after 9pm and were greeted by a kiwi that darted away into the scrub. It was an overcast, balmy (c.20°C) and wind-free night presenting perfect conditions for finding geckos. In no time at all we had our first gecko in the hand. Geckos continued to appear in swarms, and indeed this site harbours some of the best remnant populations of Forest Gecko (*Mokopirirakau granulatus*) and Elegant Gecko (*Naultinus elegans*) in the Auckland Region.

It is not unusual to find the full suite of morphological variation known in these species in a single night of surveying, from the typical grey, lichen-patterned Forest Geckos to some that have pale yellowish markings on the dorsum and others that are pale, almost white. The Elegant Geckos are a more striking lime-green with contrasting white markings or stripes along the dorsolateral lines, although some are completely uniform green. Others are not green at all, but banana-yellow!

After a few hours of catching and processing geckos, I decided I needed a break from it all and pushed into the scrub, only to be confronted with yet another delightful Elegant Gecko. This one was an adult female and although not unusual for the species, it completely lacked white markings on the body but had a distinctive white stripe along the lower jaw-line. I pulled out my camera to take some photographs and ended up chasing the gecko in and out of dense foliage as it attempted to avoid the light of my flash. I was keen to get a natural pose and refrained from trying to manipulate the gecko too much. Then suddenly, of its own accord it turned back on itself, its tail curled behind its body gently grasping the end of a small branch. I quickly repositioned the flash diffuser and fired the shutter. The shot was in the bag. I must say that I am very fond of this image as I think it captures the beauty and elegance of this species and shows why it is so aptly named.

PHOTOGRAPHIC EQUIPMENT USED

Canon 450D, Canon EF 100mm f/2.8 Macro USM Lens, 430EX II Speedlite with DIY diffuser. Adobe Photoshop Lightroom CC.

SPECIES

Starred Gecko (*Naultinus stellatus*)

PHOTOGRAPHER

Tony Jewell

STATUS

EX   EW   CR   EN   **VU**   NT   LC

LOCATION

Origin of specimen: Nelson Lakes, northern South Island

NOTES

Snout-vent length 8cm. Another diurnal and arboreal species. Like the other geckos in this group it has a prehensile tail to help with climbing. One individual was reported to have lived to the age of 47 years in captivity. Gives birth to two live young, which are born dark green with white markings, but change to their adult colouration at around two years of age.

STORY BEHIND THE PHOTO

In 2007, wildlife photographer Rod Morris and I travelled around many parts of New Zealand taking photographs in preparation for our then forthcoming book *A Photographic Guide to the Reptiles and Amphibians of New Zealand*. Aside from many field locations we also visited several reptile keepers, including Dennis Keall of Wainuiomata. On our way out to Dennis's place we collected a number of potential photographic props, an endeavour which saw us plucking random native flowers, foliage and branches from street-side specimen trees and native bush reserves across Lower Hutt. My eye was particularly taken with a flowering *Astelia* bush lily which provided an interesting combination of colours.

When we arrived at Dennis's house we were let loose among his stunning collection of native lizards and were able to cover a large selection of rare or especially beautiful specimens that would have taken many years to track down and visit in the wild. Among his diurnal green tree geckos, by far the most striking individual to my eye was this Nelson Lakes Starred Gecko. Its colours worked beautifully among the flowering *Astelia*, with some *Coprosma* foliage filling in the spaces behind.

I set it up with the idea that the flowers would provide a splash of vibrant but natural-looking colour beside the lizard in order to provide some colour depth to the image, because as striking as the gecko is on the *Astelia* foliage, the whole image would have been a little flat with just greens and whites.

Starred Geckos are arboreal foliage-dwellers that will live in a range of types of forest and shrubland, from the coast to the subalpine zone. They are typically depicted in photos among the fine-leaved shrubs such as kanuka and *Coprosma*, so I made it another goal of this image to show the species in a type of vegetation that they are not normally associated with, but is nevertheless common in their habitat and which they will undoubtedly visit from time to time. The photo was taken on Dennis's lawn on a bright sunny day, with use of shading and the background foliage to disguise the fact. While many geckos won't sit still for long in direct sunlight, Starred Geckos are primarily active by day and can spend a lot of time basking in the sun, so this individual was happy to be positioned and remain still for long enough to let me hone in on just the right photographic angle.

PHOTOGRAPHIC EQUIPMENT USED

Canon 400D with the kit lens, a high f-stop (f29) to help darken the grassy background, a low ISO (100) to keep the colours rich, and a shutter speed of 1/100s with the pop-up flash on.

SPECIES

Gulf Marbled Velvet Gecko (*Oedura bella*)

PHOTOGRAPHER

Scott Eipper

STATUS

EX   EW   CR   EN   VU   NT   **LC**

LOCATION

Mount Isa, Queensland

NOTES

Snout-vent length 9.2cm. Remained unknown to science until first described in 2016, and is one of the most recent additions to the genus *Oedura*, of which there are 15 species. All possess a striking velvet appearance and eye-catching pattern, and are arboreal, although some favour rocky crevices over bark as a refuge.

STORY BEHIND THE PHOTO

I had been travelling to Mount Isa for the past ten years with my business, Nature 4 You, conducting snake management training. During the day we were busy working, but at night we had the opportunity to see the local sites. Warm to hot weather made for interesting herping but I had heard about the lovely Gulf Marbled Velvet Geckos that were found in a few locations.

Velvet geckos can be found on trees or rocks depending on the species and the only couple we knew about were seen crossing roads. We had searched many trees and many rocks and still came up short. I spoke to a few mates for some clues but unfortunately was without luck. This, however, was going to change.

The following day one of my attendees happened to be an ecologist for one of the local mines and I asked if they had ever seen them?

They hadn't, but did bring along the herpetological records from various surveys over the past decade or so in the area. I carefully looked over the records and found three sites that had recorded the geckos before. We now had at least narrowed the search area. Later that night the four of us headed out, somewhat hopeful. Twenty minutes into the search, this stunning little juvenile was seen. I could hardly believe my luck, I yelled out with excitement to the others, To say I was happy would be an understatement. I followed it along until it stopped on the small stone at the top of a little ridge.

I had finally found my nemesis. I still have one snake to find up at 'the Isa', and much like the Gulf Marbled Velvet Gecko it's proving a challenge. The species, you wonder? The Ornate Whipsnake (*Demansia flagellatio*). One day!

PHOTOGRAPHIC EQUIPMENT USED

Nikon D300, Sigma 105 mm macro, three Nikon SB800 flashes (one camera mounted, two mounted to a Manfrotto twin flash bracket), f36, 1/250s, ISO 200, +.3 exposure bias.

SPECIES

Fringe-toed Velvet Gecko (*Oedura filicipoda*)

PHOTOGRAPHER

Lachlan Gilding

STATUS

EX   EW   CR   EN   VU   NT   **LC**

LOCATION

Kimberley Region, Western Australia

NOTES

Snout-vent length 10.5cm. As the name suggests, has elaborate fringing across toes that likely helps it navigate the rock outcrops in inhabits. Females usually produce only two or three clutches of two eggs per season. The young are born with bright wide bands, which fade as the animal matures to a uniform flecking, retaining some bands on the tail.

STORY BEHIND THE PHOTO

This species had long been high on my 'must see' list, being without doubt one of the most strikingly beautiful geckos that Australia has to offer. This particular specimen was found and photographed in 2018 whilst on a photography expedition into the remote Northern Kimberley region of Western Australia.

On this particular trip I had already come across a few adult individuals of this species, so when I caught the eye-shine of this animal I almost continued to walk on past. Luckily, I decided to have a closer look and was delighted to see that this animal was very young and was still sporting its beautiful juvenile patterning.

The Fringe-toed Velvet Gecko is at home in the impressive escarpments on the Northern Kimberley, and despite being fairly common throughout its range, its habit of sitting in extremely deep and narrow crevices can make it a hard subject to photograph. Despite all this I was happy to walk away from the trip with decent photos of both juvenile and adult specimens.

PHOTOGRAPHIC EQUIPMENT USED

Canon 7D, Canon 50mm Macro, two external flashes, one soft box.

SPECIES

Eyre Basin Beaked Gecko (*Rhynchoedura eyrensis*)

PHOTOGRAPHER

Steve Wilson

STATUS

EX EW CR EN VU NT **LC**

LOCATION

Ethabuka, Simpson Desert, Queensland

NOTES

Snout-vent length 5cm. A member of the 'beaked gecko' group of lizards, which contains six species. All are relatively small ground-dwelling geckos that are arid and semi-arid specialists feeding exclusively on termites. They spend the hot days under leaf litter or, like this specimen, in spider burrows.

STORY BEHIND THE PHOTO

I have been hooked on head-torching ever since I learned some time in the distant past that geckos' eyes reflect light. Never mind the millions of years spent evolving colours and patterns that match their backgrounds, that dim orange glow from light bouncing off its retina reveals a gecko no matter how artfully it may be concealed.

Sometimes I have a pretty good idea of what the gecko is while I am still looking at the eye-shine. Big, bright and stationary is often one of the knob-tailed geckos (*Nephrurus*). If I am in a rainforest or among cliffs or boulders, that bright still eye is probably a leaf-tailed gecko (*Saltuarius* or *Phyllurus*). If the eye-shine is on a tree trunk or rock face and it moves rapidly as I approach, then it is probably one of the *Gehyra* species. A stationary eye-shine, raised a centimetre or two above the ground, is very likely one of the stone geckos (*Diplodactylus vittatus* species complex), for they have a habit of perching on small sticks. They seem to prefer a vantage point slightly raised above the ground.

On the red sand and spinifex at Ethabuka, on the eastern edge of the Simpson Desert, I headed out with camera and flashes to see what I could find. It was a stinking hot night and a cloud of insects were buzzing in my beam, flapping into my eyes, lodging themselves in my ears and finding their way down my neck. For the umpteenth time, as a moth hit my eyeball, the thought crossed my mind that I need a pair of goggles for this sort of stuff.

A dim pinpoint of eye-shine appeared to me on an area of bare exposed sand. Keeping my beam on it as I walked towards it, the eye-shine disappeared. That's a significant clue and I think I know the culprit. Beaked geckos (*Rhynchoedura* species) and swift geckos (*Lucasium* species) spend the day in the vertical shafts of invertebrate burrows. They seem particularly fond of wolf spider holes. If they have not fully emerged when the torch beam illuminates them, they often reverse back down the hole. Hence the disappearing eye-shine.

Sure enough, when I reached the spot, there was a beaked gecko still quite visible but just below the entrance to the hole. It was ready to back down further and I was able to take a single shot before it reversed from view. I used a master flash mounted on the camera and a hand-held slave aimed down the burrow. After I had gone it would have re-emerged to hunt termites. And I have my in situ shot of a secretive desert lizard at the entrance to its retreat. I call that a win-win.

PHOTOGRAPHIC EQUIPMENT USED

Canon EOS 6D with 100 mm lens, f32, 1/100s, ISO 100, 580EX master flash with 430EX slave flash.

SPECIES

Northern Spiny-tailed Gecko (*Strophurus ciliaris ciliaris*)

PHOTOGRAPHER

Jules Farquhar

STATUS

EX EW CR EN VU NT **LC**

LOCATION

Flinders Ranges, South Australia

NOTES

Snout-vent length 9cm. When threatened they exude a noxious sticky fluid from the glands in their tail. Predominantly arboreal, inhabiting trees, shrubs and spinifex clumps. Forage for insects at night both in shrubbery and on the ground. Once mature, females may lay six to eight clutches in a single season.

STORY BEHIND THE PHOTO

In December 2017, some friends and I set out on a ten-day trip to look for reptiles across north-west Victoria, the Flinders Ranges, Lake Eyre and the Coober Pedy region. We started the trip well at a salt lake in the Victorian Mallee, where we found several Lined Earless Dragons (*Tympanocryptis lineata*).

We then spent the whole of 27 December driving from Victoria to the Flinders Ranges. It was over 40°C and the air conditioner in the Landcruiser was broken. By night we had made it to the Flinders and were driving down a rocky track heading towards Lake Frome, where we planned on camping for the night. We were stopping every few hundred metres to spotlight through the dried-out creeklines for gecko eye-shine. But all we could find were Bynoe's Geckos (*Heteronotia binoei*) on the ground and Variable Dtellas (*Gehyra versicolor*) on the trees. At 11pm, after several hours of finding only common geckos, and having to change a flat tyre, we followed a flicker of eye-shine to a large Northern Spiny-tailed Gecko perched on a low hanging tree branch in a creek. We were surprised to see one here, because they had not been widely recorded in the Flinders Ranges.

Suddenly, I began sweating profusely. Not because of the prized gecko find, but because I had eaten a questionable pasta salad earlier that day at an outback roadhouse, and the effects of food poisoning were taking hold. There was no time to be sick, because this gecko needed to be photographed. Feeling nauseous, I quickly grabbed my camera and started setting up the flashes. I struggled to stay upright as I walked through the bush looking for a nice stick to photograph the gecko on. I took several full-body photos of the gecko when it started cleaning its lidless-eyes with its tongue, so I leaned in closer to take a headshot of it in action. I wanted to time the photo such that its tongue had just left the mouth, but had not yet reached the eye. For this photo I decided to turn the power of my right flash down low, while holding the left flash out in front of the subject at slightly higher power. This gives the side of the lizard's face more contrast and makes the image more dynamic than it would be if both flashes were fired at equal power and coming from the same direction. With the aid of external flashes, one has full control over lighting position, direction and intensity – all of which have considerable influence on the final image. I have found that the biggest leaps forward in developing my photography have been related to new ways of positioning flashes, rather than the camera settings used.

PHOTOGRAPHIC EQUIPMENT USED

Canon EOS 70D, Canon EF-S 60mm f/2.8 USM macro lens, f/9, 1/250s, ISO 100, RAW. The camera's built-in flash was used to trigger two Canon Speedlite flashes with diffusion softboxes: one hand-held and one on a Manfrotto 330B Macro Flash Bracket. Minor adjustments to exposure were made using Adobe Lightroom.

SPECIES

Golden-tailed Gecko (*Strophurus taenicauda*)

PHOTOGRAPHER

Steve Wilson

STATUS

EX   EW   CR   EN   VU   NT   **LC**

LOCATION

Lake Broadwater, Queensland

NOTES

Snout-vent length 7.5cm. One of our most striking lizards. Members of the genus *Strophurus* have the ability to squirt a harmless smelly fluid from their tails. This is used as a deterrent against birds and other predations whilst they are perching in shrubs.

STORY BEHIND THE PHOTO

Call me vain, but this image of a Golden-tailed Gecko actually includes a self-portrait. The gecko is one of the most photogenic species in Australia, thanks to that fiery red eye and the vivid gold slash along the top of the tail, all set against a backdrop of pale grey with a mosaic of sharply contrasting black spots.

They are reasonably common in dry forests featuring a combination of eucalypts, native pines, and sometimes brigalow. Fortunately it takes me only three or four hours' drive from home to Lake Broadwater where they occur.

I had a need for several different images of Golden-tailed Geckos for some book projects I was working on, so I went out for a weekend to find some. The geckos are mainly arboreal, often selecting perches on slender branches. They have strong eye-shine in the head-torch beam, are generally slow-moving and often freeze when illuminated, so it did not take long to find a couple in a stand of native pines that I had visited before.

It was during the course of taking the various shots I wanted – climbing along branches, perching among foliage and some close-ups facing the camera – that I pondered on the reflective nature of that fabulous eye. Suppose I was to get in close and point a flash backwards at myself? Would that work out as a weird herpetological self-portrait? That is the beauty of digital photography. In my decades of using slide film, the time span between pressing the shutter and viewing the result was days at best and usually weeks. There was no ability to instantly make the necessary adjustments in the middle of a photo session. And of course every time I took a picture it would cost money.

It took a few attempts to get the sort of thing I was after. The gecko was photographed in shaded daylight using a tripod. A master flash mounted on the camera was directed upwards, away from the gecko but sufficient to trigger a second slave flash. How best to angle the slave aimed at me? How close should my face be to the gecko in order to actually get my dial in the picture? Was I handsome enough to even bother?

I think I managed to deal with the first two questions to achieve the results I was after. Regarding the last question, I guess that's up to the viewer to decide.

PHOTOGRAPHIC EQUIPMENT USED

Canon EOS 30D with 100 mm lens, f14, 1/2s, ISO 100. Daylight with flash turned back towards photographer.

SPECIES

Harlequin Gecko (*Tukutuku rakiurae*)

PHOTOGRAPHER

Dylan van Winkel

STATUS

EX   EW   CR   **EN**   VU   NT   LC

LOCATION

Stewart Island

NOTES

Snout-vent length 7cm. A real cold-weather specialist and one of the southernmost gecko species in the world.

STORY BEHIND THE PHOTO

If there is one species of New Zealand lizard that gets most herpetologists completely excited, it must be the unique, striking and gorgeous Harlequin Gecko of Stewart Island. Planning a trip to see this species is like planning a wedding, which involves a complicated and painstaking process of organising travel, accommodation and food provisions, praying for good weather, deciding on the most appropriate outfit to wear, learning to restrain your emotions and tears of joy following initial eye-contact, choosing the right words for your celebratory speech, and importantly practicing your dance moves so as not to embarrass yourself in front of your peers.

Two colleagues and I began preparing for a trip to see this species months in advance. On 9 February 2018 we boarded the ferry at Bluff, with hiking packs jammed full of warm garments (this is one of the most southerly distributed geckos in the world), camera gear and food. The journey across the Foveaux Strait is often rough; however, this time we were in for a relatively smooth sailing.

We disembarked in the small seaside town of Oban, and set off for the local Department of Conservation office to register our intentions, grab UHF radios and discuss logistics. Our journey took us along the west coast by boat before darting inland to be dropped at the start of an unmarked track. From here we hiked up through closed-canopy forest before emerging into the herb fields that dominate the alpine zone. We moved over the soft ground, examining every bit of vegetation for movement. It was overcast with very little wind and quite warm (c.14°C) – well, warm considering that Harlequin Geckos are known to remain active at temperatures below 5°C. Conditions were perfect for detecting this species, and I distinctly remember systematically combing the short vegetation with my fingertips thinking that surely these geckos cannot survive in such low-growing herbs, especially in winter when frosts or even snow cover the ground. Then suddenly, boisterous squeals of joy, manic cackles of laughter and long howls of satisfaction as my mate popped out from behind a small shrub with tears in his eyes, dancing for joy and fumbling his celebratory sentences. He opened his hand and all three of us nearly fainted. In front of us was the most glorious gecko I had ever seen, like an oil painting of greens, yellows, reds, and orange brush-strokes arranged longitudinally in a herringbone pattern that extended from the animal's head to the tip of its tail. It was rather small (c.55 SVL) but none of us cared… it was a HARLEQUIN GECKO!

We spent the following three days finding and photographing these amazing geckos and the novelty never wore off because every individual was marked and coloured so differently. The camouflage against the background herbs was amazing and the geckos would literally disappear in front of your eyes only to reappear when they made their next movement. Despite the logistical challenges of getting to the site, and nearly freezing to death overnight in wet clothes in a flooded tent, I would do it all again in a heartbeat.

PHOTOGRAPHIC EQUIPMENT USED

Canon 450D, Canon EF-S 60mm f/2.8 Macro USM, 430EX II Speedlite with DIY diffuser. Adobe Photoshop Lightroom CC.

SPECIES

Javelin Delma (*Delma concinna*)

PHOTOGRAPHER

Steve Wilson

STATUS

EX   EW   CR   EN   VU   NT   **LC**

LOCATION

Between Jurien and Green Head, Western Australia

NOTES

Snout-vent length 11cm. Lives in dense low vegetation and the thick leaf litter below. When startled they are able to use a springing motion to escape predators, and herpetologists.

STORY BEHIND THE PHOTO

I've spent many hours looking for Javelin Delmas in the complex heaths between Jurien and Green Head on the lower west coast of Western Australia. The area is a hot-spot for members of the family Pygopodidae, probably supporting more species than anywhere else in Australia.

It is easy to get distracted in that striking habitat, considered among the floral wonders of the world.

In spring it is a kaleidoscope of colour as the immense variety of plants, competing for space on the nutrient-poor sandy ground, are in full bloom. They include woolly bush, prostrate Banksias, kangaroo paws, orchids and a variety of peas and tea trees, nearly all of them endemic to the south-west. The Javelin Delma is most at home in this dense low vegetation, among the stems, branches, foliage and flowers. A diurnal lizard, it is often seen basking atop vegetation up to a metre above the ground. At up to 40cm long and no thicker than a pencil, with a tail about four times the length of the body, it reminds me of a hyper-alert, exceedingly swift, animated shoelace! I've probably seen a couple of dozen of them in the wild as they are reasonably common on a pleasantly warm spring morning, but rarely have I had more than a fleeting glimpse. As often as not the lizard has vanished, a grey blur then gone, before my mind registers that I ever saw it. This sometimes has the strange effect of causing me to wonder if it was there at all.

The species was originally described by Arnold Kluge in 1974 as *Aclys concinna*, which translates to 'beautiful spear'. The long snout and extremely slender body reminded Dr Kluge of a spear, with a superb striped grey colour which he found attractive. Had Dr Kluge seen a live one in the wild when he named the lizard, its appearance and behaviour would certainly have reinforced his apt selection of names.

I really wanted to take an image that captures several elements of this legless lizard. The first is its elegant form, so slender, graceful and subtly patterned. I also wanted it on location to showcase the floral abundance of its habitat, those uniquely Western Australian shrubs and flowers. And I wanted to avoid using flash in keeping with its diurnal habits. Getting the result I wanted made all those irritating ticks I had to remove after every visit worth the trouble.

PHOTOGRAPHIC EQUIPMENT USED

Canon EOS 30D with 100 mm lens, f9, 1/160s, ISO 400.

SPECIES

Common Scaly-foot (*Pygopus lepidopodus*)

PHOTOGRAPHER

Rob Valentic

STATUS

~~EX~~ ~~EW~~ ~~CR~~ ~~EN~~ ~~VU~~ ~~NT~~ **LC**

LOCATION

Fowlers Bay, South Australia

NOTES

Snout-vent length 27.5cm. Largest in south Queensland, where total length of 1m possible, almost three-quarters of which is tail. Highly variable in colour, and the one shown here is rather bright! Lays up to four clutches per season with two eggs in each.

STORY BEHIND THE PHOTO

Arid South Australia has some breathtaking landscapes. Accommodating the state's rich herpetofauna into those landscapes with wide-angle lenses has provided me with some of my most treasured images and memories. This one is right up there.

Fowlers Bay is situated on the eastern edge of the Nullarbor Plain. It is a place that I am constantly drawn to due to the contrasting combination of towering white sand dunes flanking a turquoise sea and the vastness of the surrounding arid salinas resulting in a rich colour palette. As the region is largely unpopulated, it offers the kind of tranquility and solitude that I crave.

This particular trip was in late September 2014. We celebrated our daughter's first birthday on this very day with a cake, candle, party hats and balloons tied to shrubs. While she took a nap I went for a stroll with camera gear in tow along the base of the coastal dunes. I noted that the local Dugites and scaly-foots were very active as they sought out potential mates and rivals, particularly along the zone between the dunes and samphire flats flanking the salt pans. The weather was perfect and in the low twenties. As the afternoon wore on, I spotted a strikingly marked Common Scaly-foot cruising slowly along the base of a dune. I temporarily restrained the lizard and looked for a location that would potentially compliment this spectacular reptile.

The light was improving by the minute and the calm conditions were desirable, in that the surrounding vegetation would not be marred by motion blur, the lizard would not be startled when buffeted by a sudden wind gust, and my lens coating would not get a sandblasting. I quickly settled on a scene that through the viewer appeared spectacular without the addition of a subject. I was very fortunate to have pleasing altocumulus cloud formations falling within the frame to further balance the scene. The punch of vibrant colour from the flowering pigface in the background was really the cherry on top.

I took some test shots to ensure my exposure was correct and gently draped the lizard onto a chenopod. I coaxed him into a pleasing posture positioned against the sun so that he was backlit to an extent. Unlike the majority of reptiles I deal with he remained motionless, and after several quick shots and an obligatory screen check we were done. I then ran him 50m back to the site of our initial encounter and wished him well as we parted ways. I was very content as I made my way back to our tent and so grateful for that interaction, the ideal weather and Fowlers Bay for turning it all on. It is a day that I won't ever forget and I'll cherish those images of these scaly-foots for as long as I've got. Oh did I mention it was also my daughter's first birthday?

PHOTOGRAPHIC EQUIPMENT USED

Canon 5D Mark III DSLR, 15/2.8 Canon Fisheye Lens, camera mounted, diffused external Canon Speedlite Flash. Adobe Photoshop Elements 2018 with RAW plugin.

SPECIES

Closed-litter Rainbow Skink (*Carlia longipes*)

PHOTOGRAPHER

Jiri Herout

STATUS

EX EW CR EN VU NT **LC**

LOCATION

North-east Queensland

NOTES

Snout-vent length 6.8cm. A member of the genus *Carlia*, which contains 50 species and is one of the most successful and widespread groups of lizards in Australia, occupying most of the country.

STORY BEHIND THE PHOTO

On a visit to the outback in Queensland we found this great spot along a river beside a magnificent waterfall. We were happy to jump in for a swim as we had seen some Aboriginal people swimming there and trusted that they knew it would be a safe place.

After approximately 10 minutes in the water, I suddenly and luckily spotted a very nice skink. I jumped out for my camera and 70–200mm lens. Soon I had taken some very nice photos but I still felt that there could be an opportunity for something better. So I changed to a 100mm macro lens and approached the skink more closely at a very slow pace so as not to scare it. Luckily, the skink itself was concentrated and calm as it was spying on flies for a potential meal. That's how I obtained this beautiful picture of a Closed-litter Rainbow Skink basking in the sun on the river bank. It has a beautiful pattern and when you look closely at its body it shines with rainbow colours.

This is one of the many small leaf litter-dwelling skinks found in the rainforest of north-eastern Queensland. Growing up to 10cm, it commonly feeds on small arthropods that inhabit the forest floor. Males have beautiful orange-red colour on the flanks during the breeding season.

PHOTOGRAPHIC EQUIPMENT USED

Canon EOS 5D Mark 3, f4, 1/640s, ISO 125. Focal length 100mm.

SPECIES

Yellow-blotched Forest Skink (*Concinnia tigrinus*)

PHOTOGRAPHER

Steve Swanson

STATUS

EX EW CR EN VU NT **LC**

LOCATION

Mount Hypipamee National Park, Queensland

NOTES

Snout-vent length 8.5cm. The genus *Concinnia* has eight members that are diverse in appearance. Some species meet the description of 'small brown skink', while others are patterned with beautiful hues of yellow and blue. One member that lives in the wet tropics has extraordinary keeled scales.

STORY BEHIND THE PHOTO

Mount Hypipamee National Park is an area of high-altitude rainforest about 20km south of Atherton, north Queensland. From the car park, a 400m walking track winds through the forest to a viewing platform above a water-filled volcanic crater.

If you are very lucky you might encounter a Lumholtz's Tree-Kangaroo or a Southern Cassowary along this track. I've also found this to be a good location for Yellow-blotched Forest Skinks. They can be observed basking in dappled sunlight at the entrance of their refuge, usually a hollow or fissure in the trunk of a large tree. They are accustomed to people walking past on the track so it is often possible to move in close for a photograph. I took this image while walking the track one afternoon in October 2012.

PHOTOGRAPHIC EQUIPMENT USED

Pentax K10D, Pentax 90mm macro, f19, flash sync speed 1/180s, external flashgun mounted on camera hotshoe. Some minor adjustments to the image using Photoshop.

SPECIES

Blue-tailed Skink (*Cryptoblepahrus egeriae*)

PHOTOGRAPHER

Hal Cogger

STATUS

EX **EW** CR EN VU NT LC

LOCATION

Near Flying Fish Cove, Christmas Island

NOTES

Snout-vent length: 4.3cm. In 2009 only 66 animals were found in the wild, subsequently leading to Parks Australia collecting the remaining individuals for captive breeding. This species would become extinct without the continued efforts of ex situ conservation. The exact threats are unknown, but many believe that the various introduced species on Christmas Island led to the skink's rapid decline. By 2019 there was a thriving captive population of more than 1,500 individuals, and reintroduction to nearby predator-free islands had begun with the hope of creating self-sustaining populations.

STORY BEHIND THE PHOTO

This little snake-eyed skink is endemic to Christmas Island where, like most of the 23 *Cryptoblepharus* species found in Australia, it is an agile, basking skink that suns itself on walls, fences and trees. When I first encountered it, it reminded me instantly of the several species of small, bright blue-tailed *Emoia* skinks that are found so commonly on most Pacific islands.

On our first survey of the reptiles of Christmas Island in 1979, Blue-tailed Skinks were very abundant. We found them on town buildings, walls and gardens, on coastal coral limestone cliffs and deep within rainforest wherever the sun penetrated the floor of the forest for extended periods. They also occupied old mined areas that consisted of bare limestone pinnacles left after the phosphate-rich soils had been removed, and over which grass and vines had grown.

This photograph was taken in May 1979. It shows a skink basking at the base of a coconut palm in the garden of the house we had been assigned for our stay in the settlement on the north coast of the island.

Following the unintended introduction to Christmas Island in the mid-1980s of the Oriental Wolf Snake (*Lycodon capucinus*), this little skink became increasingly rare. In 1998, on another survey of the island, we saw fewer than a dozen Blue-tailed skinks in two weeks, while in 2008 I saw only four wild skinks. They had completely disappeared from the town area where 20 years earlier they had been so abundant. However by this time Christmas Island National Park had taken some specimens into captivity in an attempt to increase their numbers by captive breeding, in the hope that the cause(s) of their decline might be identified and then ameliorated, and the skink reintroduced. To date several thousand skinks have been bred in captivity at Taronga Zoo in Sydney and on Christmas Island, to be used in reintroduction trials. None survive in the wild.

PHOTOGRAPHIC EQUIPMENT USED

Leica 1G camera with attached mirror reflex housing and using a 65mm macro Leitz Elmar lens on 64ASA Kodachrome film with twin flashes. Age and projection dust and scratches were removed post-scanning using Photoshop CS6.

SPECIES

Central Pygmy Spiny-tailed Skink (*Egernia eos*)

PHOTOGRAPHER

Max Jackson

STATUS

EX EW CR EN VU NT **LC**

LOCATION

Warburton Region, Western Australia

NOTES

Snout-vent length 10cm. First described as a new species in 2011. Known from scattered records across its range and appears to be locally common at known localities.

STORY BEHIND THE PHOTO

The genus *Egernia* has always been a favourite of mine, in particular those species that possess spiny-tails. The Central Pygmy Spiny-tailed Skink is restricted to a small area in the Central Deserts where it spends most of its days in the cracks and crevices of rock escarpments and hollow logs. Passing through their small range in October 2018, I made sure to put some time aside to see and hopefully photograph one of these cryptic skinks.

After about an hour of searching I was lucky enough to catch a glimpse of one of their orange eyes peeking out at me through a crack in a large hollow log on the ground. I decided to wait and hope the lizard would come out of its own accord and had been sitting on the ground leaning against a hollowed out stag for about 20 minutes without any success when I heard a scratching sound coming from the tree that I was leaning against. Looking up I saw that another *Egernia eos* had crawled out of an opening and was now sitting out in the open getting some sun right above my head. Not believing my own luck I managed to get a few images of this rarely seen species before it wriggled its prickly body back into the safety of its tree hollow.

PHOTOGRAPHIC EQUIPMENT USED

Canon 7D Mark II, Tamron 90mm, Twin Flash Canon EX 480, f13, 1/200s, ISO 250, 90mm. Edited using Lightroom.

SPECIES

Gidgee Skink (*Egernia stokesii zellingi*)

PHOTOGRAPHER

Jules Farquhar

STATUS

EX   EW   CR   EN   VU   NT   **LC**

LOCATION

Flinders Ranges, South Australia

NOTES

Snout-vent length 19.4cm. Species in the genus *Egernia* form complex social structures. This species and others are being studied by scientists hoping to understand the evolution of sociality and family life. Due to their interesting behaviour they are now one of the most popular pet skinks.

STORY BEHIND THE PHOTO

Like most of my fondest memories of looking for reptiles, this story begins in outback South Australia, in the Flinders Ranges. It was 20 January 2016 and I had spent the past three days clambering around the ancient ridgelines of the Flinders. This was in the days when I was foolhardy enough to herp in Stubbies, so my legs were terribly sunburnt and covered in wounds from accidental collisions with the abrasive metamorphic rocks. There are endless reasons why a naturalist would endure such circumstances, but for a herpetologist visiting the Flinders Ranges, my rationale was simple: find Red-barred Dragons, Tawny Dragons, Masked Rock-skinks and Gidgee Skinks. I found these four lizards when I visited the region three years earlier, but I only managed to photograph the ubiquitous Tawny Dragon at Wilpena Pound. So the objective of this trip was to photograph others.

I was driving along an unsealed track heading east from Blinman, stopping where rocky creeks and ridges intersected the track to scan for signs of reptiles. I had just left Wilpena Pound, where I photographed numerous Tawny Dragons and saw several Masked Rock-skinks. So now I was hoping to find the particular ridgeline where I caught a fleeting glimpse of both Red-barred Dragons and Gidgee Skinks three years earlier. But, alas, due to the time elapsed I couldn't quite remember what the ridge looked like and one can only remember so many ridges in their life! After an hour of driving down the track, the fabled ridgeline appeared. I immediately started searching the ridge and noticed the skyline was dotted with the silhouettes of Red-barred Dragons perched on the highest parts of rocks. Getting photos of them proved to be relatively simple, so I turned my attention to the Gidgee Skink.

This particular ridgeline was teeming with Gidgee Skinks. However, they would retreat to the nearest crevice at the slightest provocation. It is practically impossible to get them out of a crevice, on account of their spinose bodies. After several hours in the 40°C heat, with no Gidgee Skink in hand, I went and laid beneath a Mulga tree in an ephemeral creekline to try cool down and stave off heat stroke. As I lay beneath the tree, I looked up at the ridge thinking of how I would get a photo of these elusive lizards. I knew I would have to do something different. So, with the little remaining energy I had, I walked over to a large rock at the side of the track and flipped it. Lo and behold, there was a Gidgee Skink. I placed the lizard on a rock and started taking photos. A storm began to roll in, which provided a dramatic background of clouds and more comfortable conditions to photograph under. I find that *Egernia* species are fairly easy to photograph, so this was a short photo session.

PHOTOGRAPHIC EQUIPMENT USED

Canon EOS 70D, Canon EF-S 10–22mm f/3.5-4.5 USM lens at 17mm focal length, f14, 1/200s, ISO 250, RAW. The camera's built-in flash was used to trigger two Canon Speedlite flashes on a Manfrotto 330B Macro Flash Bracket to illuminate the front of the subject. Minor adjustments to exposure were made using Adobe Lightroom.

SPECIES

Mangrove Skink (*Emoia atrocostata*)

PHOTOGRAPHER

Hal Cogger

STATUS

EX EW CR EN VU NT **LC**

LOCATION

The Blowholes, south coast of Christmas Island, Indian Ocean

NOTES

Snout-vent length 8.5cm. At home in northern Queensland, this small skink is semi-aquatic and known to forage in tidal pools. Also found in Papua New Guinea, Vanuatu, the Solomon Islands, Indonesia, Malaysia, the Philippines, Vietnam, Taiwan and the Ryukyu Islands.

Listed as Least Concern throughout its range, although the Christmas Island population is believed to be extinct – a harsh reminder that each ecosystem is in a delicate balance and the introduction of a species can have devastating consequences.

STORY BEHIND THE PHOTO

In 1979 Ross Sadlier and I travelled to Christmas Island, c.350km south of Java, to carry out an Australian Museum reptile survey of the island for the Australian National Parks and Wildlife Service. We arrived on Christmas Island after two weeks surveying the herps of the Cocos (Keeling) Islands, where we had left behind a group of small, low sandy islets arrayed around the edge of the large atoll, with a herp fauna of four species – three common, widespread oceanic geckos and the ubiquitous Flowerpot Snake or Brahminy Blind Snake (*Indotyphlops braminus*) – all likely to have been introduced by human agency after settlement of the atoll in 1827.

Christmas Island, by comparison, is a large raised coral island (13,470ha) atop an ancient volcano. Originally covered by dense rainforest on the plateau, and with steep coastal limestone terraces, about a third of the island has been mined for its rich guano-derived phosphate deposits. Around two-thirds of the island, including much of the original rainforest, are now set aside as a national park. Six species of reptiles, five of them endemic, occurred at the time of settlement in 1889, while an additional five species have since been established on the island.

On our survey, in 1979, three of these species were new records – a skink, a gecko and a blind snake –all apparently chance introductions by human agency since World War II when the island was occupied by the Japanese.

We conducted another survey of Christmas Island for the Australian Government in 1998, but this species – commonly seen during our 1979 survey – was not found. It is one of two skinks of the genus *Emoia* found on Christmas Island. Whereas one – the Forest Skink (*Emoia nativitatis*) – was largely confined to rainforest, this species is largely restricted to the coastal edges – the coral limestone pinnacles and cliffs that surround Christmas Island and are broken only by occasional sandy beaches. In 1979 this skink, considered to be conspecific with various island populations ranging from about Singapore through Indonesia to the western Pacific, and all of which also occupy mostly littoral habitats, was common though hard to catch. However we saw none in 1999 and the last specimen seen alive on the island was in September 2009. This unique, isolated island population is now regarded as extinct.

PHOTOGRAPHIC EQUIPMENT USED

Leica 1G camera with attached mirror reflex housing and using a 65mm macro Leitz Elmar lens on 100 ASA Kodachrome. Image taken among a field of razor-sharp coral rock pinnacles where I was preoccupied with not losing my footing or the skink while saving my camera from the saltwater spray and mist that engulfed us with each breaking wave.

SPECIES

Blue Mountains Water Skink (*Eulamprus leuraensis*)

PHOTOGRAPHER

Jiri Herout

STATUS

EX EW CR **EN** VU NT LC

LOCATION

Blue Mountains, New South Wales

NOTES

Snout-vent length 7cm. Genetic studies have shown that this species has occupied swamps in the Blue Mountains for more than 2 million years. It is totally reliant on the peat swamps in the mid- to upper Blue Mountains for its survival.

STORY BEHIND THE PHOTO

One of the most memorable days of my life was 16 October 2016. It was a very hot day in the whole of New South Wales and it was just the beginning of the spring season. I would never have imagined that I was going to photograph one of the rarest skinks in Australia.

I had visited the Blue Mountains many times before, hoping that I would spot this skink in its natural habitat. On that day I got very lucky. I forgot my full photography gear, which was languishing at home, and the only camera I had with me was a Canon 5D Mark 3 and 17–40mm lens.

This water skink is only found in a small area of the Blue Mountains. As the name implies, it lives near water, and this is where I spotted it. I was in a beautiful valley crossed by a small stream near the Three Sisters area. The grass was already dried and a lot of wooden sticks were covering this precious source of water.

Out of nowhere, I saw this small and beautifully coloured skink. At first I did not even realise that it was my long-searched-for Blue Mountains Water Skink. And then, after a short while, it hit me that my dreams had come true. I cannot even describe the happiness and excitement I felt while I was photographing it.

PHOTOGRAPHIC EQUIPMENT USED

Canon EOS 5D Mark 3, Canon 580 Mark 2 flash with two external diffusers – one on the lens and one on top of the flash – f13, 1/200s, ISO 100. Focal length 40mm.

SPECIES

Dreeite Water Skink (*Eulamprus tympanum marniae*)

PHOTOGRAPHER

Rob Valentic

STATUS

EX EW **CR** EN VU NT LC

LOCATION

Nerrin Nerrin, Victoria

NOTES

Snout-vent length 9.7cm. A striking skink that inhabits the margins of lakes in basalt lava flows in a western lakes district of south-western Victoria. Habitat loss, degradation and fragmentation are contributing to the decline of this species, which is now extinct at two localities where it used to occur.

STORY BEHIND THE PHOTO

Unlike the widespread and ubiquitous nominate form, this boldly marked subspecies of the Southern Water Skink is confined to a small area.

In mid-January 2015, I embarked on a solo trip to search several freshwater lakes around Nerrin Nerrin. I planned to locate and photograph Dreeite Water Skink with a wide-angle lens, in an attempt to show the skink within the context of its immediate habitat. I reached the lakes around mid-morning and noted that the shoreline was largely featureless from a skink's perspective, with the exception of a low and narrow basalt ridge abutting the shoreline on the opposite side. As I walked closer I saw numerous boulder heaps accumulated along the base of this ridge. The result of collapsed lava tunnels, these act as important refugia for these skinks. Within the crumbled labyrinth the microclimate remains cool and damp, providing a sanctuary from droughts and excessive heat.

Upon entering the rock piles, I was not confident of seeing any basking skinks yet as it was quite cold. As the day warmed up a few heads started to protrude from the many fissures and crevices along the ridge. I was lucky to witness this emergence event and it is how I intended to time my visit to this site. The adult skinks are very flighty once active and usually retreat well before they are in range of the camera. Mornings like this provide the best opportunity to make a close approach, because some individuals are reluctant to vacate the warmth of their basking site.

Eventually I concentrated solely on a particularly striking male that was basking on an elevated ledge overlooking the water. I was so thrilled when I had him in hand and complete, following a 15-minute commando approach! Temporarily housing him in a container I quickly scouted the immediate area for an appealing angle that would offer a strong composition in which to showcase this beautiful skink. I walked over to where the outcrop petered out a little and where there were exposed patches of gravel on the shoreline. This location offered some safeguard in the sense that I'd have a chance to recapture the subject in the event that he bolted while I had both hands full of camera.

Inspecting the scene in the viewfinder, I was satisfied that all of the criteria for the habitat requirements of the skink were included. After the mandatory exposure checks and test shots I positioned the most obliging subject on a stone in an elevated stance, in an attempt to highlight the distinctive yellow and black throat markings that distinguish the subspecies. I took three shots, and upon checking these, I was elated with the result. I always release any wild subject as quickly as possible and this skink was no exception. I ran him back to the ledge and placed him on it, whereupon he continued to bask, seemingly unperturbed by the encounter. The best outcome possible.

PHOTOGRAPHIC EQUIPMENT USED

Canon 5D Mark III DSLR, Canon 15/2.8 Fisheye lens, hotshoe mounted diffused external Speedlite. Adobe Photoshop Elements 2018 with Raw Plugin.

SPECIES

Southern Water Skink (*Eulamprus tympanum tympanum*)

PHOTOGRAPHER

Benjamin Stubbs

STATUS

EX EW CR EN VU NT **LC**

LOCATION

Sunbury, Victoria

NOTES

Snout-vent length 9.7cm. As the name implies, usually resides next to creeks or other water bodies and feeds on invertebrates, tadpoles, frogs and small skinks. Once fed, the metabolic rate increases to more than double the rate prior to feeding and remains elevated for up to 48 hours. This is common for frequent feeders. Bears live young in mid- to late summer. The female selects the sex of the young by regulating her body temperature – she does this by managing the amount of time she spends basking. When male populations are low, clutches tend to have more male young, and when female numbers are low clutches have more females.

STORY BEHIND THE PHOTO

Water skinks have always been a favourite reptile of mine. Usually I encounter them briefly as they drop down into the rocks, following their already planned escape route, but when you're quiet and still for a few minutes they will emerge and you can watch them hunt and bask. They're pretty downright awesome.

This image was taken on 6 October 2018, in situ along Jackson Creek. This particular skink was one of probably ten I saw in around a five-minute period along the creek system I was walking. It is a very rocky area providing many hiding places for these skinks to move around freely but be back in safety in the blink of an eye if needed.

I noticed this one perched on the rock ledge, around 1.5m off the ground, and I decided to slowly try and approach it in what I thought was a foolish hope of it not retreating to safety. To my surprise, as I clambered over rocks, balancing my camera, softbox and bag, this little guy did not move.

This was a surprisingly difficult situation for photography: standing on the peak of a single rock, balancing with a rock outcrop over my head meaning that I was slumped in an uncomfortable position, making it all the more surprising that the skink didn't take off straight away.

I was lucky enough to be able to take some initial shots and then recompose, and it was not until I got a little too greedy with how close I was that the skink darted back into the gaps in the rocks you can see in the image.

Shooting so close to reptiles, in most cases in situ shots are not possible. So it's always nice to have a rare interaction, especially with such a flighty species, to be able to capture it on camera without first having to handle it. It does mean that the composition isn't always what you want, but in this case I caught a nice pose with the water flowing in the background. You can have some amazing experiences with our native reptiles.

PHOTOGRAPHIC EQUIPMENT USED

Nikon D7500, Tamron 10-24 F/3.5-4.5 Di II VC, Nikon Sb-700 speedlight through 40cm soft box. Minor lighting adjustments made in Adobe Lightroom.

SPECIES

Black Mountain Skink (*Liburnascincus scirtetis*)

PHOTOGRAPHER

Shane Black

STATUS

EX EW CR EN **VU** NT LC

LOCATION

Cooktown, far north Queensland

NOTES

Snout-vent length 6.4cm. Inhabits an area of 6.2km^2 on Black Mountain, Queensland. The genus *Liburnascincus* consists of saxicoline (rock-dwelling) skinks that are restricted to north-east Australia. One widespread species is the Outcrop Rock Skink (*L. mundivensis*), while two other localised species also occur – Coen Rainbow Skink (*L. coensis*) and Bamboo Range Rock Skink (*L. artemis*).

STORY BEHIND THE PHOTO

The Black Mountain Skink is a small lizard endemic to the Cooktown region of far north Queensland. Within that region it is confined to the granite boulders of Black Mountain, from which it derives its name.

I headed up the coast to Cooktown in late September, 2015 with the aim of getting some decent images of this species. I had already been to this area many times in the past, but had never put the effort in to get some quality pics.

I arrived at Black Mountain late in the afternoon hoping that the skinks would still be active. From past experience I knew that they often remain out until sunset, but this particular day was overcast and a bit on the cool side. As I was setting my camera up, I could see the odd skink scurrying over the boulders and knew I'd be able to have a crack at a few pics before dark.

As I made my way across the boulders juvenile skinks were jumping from rock to rock, nervous by my presence. Then I spotted a full-grown adult sitting proudly atop his treasured piece of real estate.

I slowly edged closer hoping that he would hold his ground. I needn't have worried because this individual showed little fear and watched me inquisitively.

Due to the poor light I had to raise the ISO, but as always I was very conscious of making sure my image portrayed the conditions accurately and I wanted this photo to represent the late evening in which it was taken. I had only snapped a single shot when a flying-fox flew low overhead startling the skink, and forcing him to dart for cover. Every photographer knows the feeling when a subject takes off earlier than hoped, and then looking at your few images, or single image in my case, and hoping you have something usable. On top of this, I was also using an extremely 'soft' old Sigma lens. For non-photographers soft means a lens of poor quality that has trouble delivering a sharp image. But to my delight, when I viewed the shot I found the combination of poor light, bokeh (out of focus areas), ISO, and soft lens actually added to the 'feel' of this particular image.

PHOTOGRAPHIC EQUIPMENT USED

Nikon D800, Sigma 400mm lens, f8, 1/250s, ISO 500. No photo editing software.

SPECIES

Great Desert Skink (*Liopholis kintorei*)

PHOTOGRAPHER

Max Jackson

STATUS

EX   EW   CR   EN   **VU**   NT   LC

LOCATION

Tanami Desert, Northern Territory

NOTES

Snout-vent length 18.7cm. Once common across the Gibson Desert, Great Victoria Desert and Great Sandy Desert, but now lost in these localities. Possible causes of these local extinctions include altered fire regimes, predation by feral cats and foxes, burrow displacement and introduced rabbits. In the year 2000 it was reported that wildfires affected about 30 per cent of the Tanami Desert bioregion. At the time it was estimated that up to one third of this species' population was living in the region. Once fire clears all the surface vegetation the skinks may be unable to survive in an environment where no habitat remains to provide food and shelter.

STORY BEHIND THE PHOTO

In late September 2018, I had to drive from Brisbane to Broome to assist in an annual survey of a Kimberley population of Freshwater Crocodiles. Naturally I created a route that would allow me to see a variety of new species along the way, with Great Desert Skink being high on the target list. This species had always intrigued me. Despite its large size, this skink is rarely seen and even more scarcely photographed due to its cryptic nature. Living in large communal burrow systems in red sandy deserts, they shelter away from the heat and are most active during the dawn-to-dusk period.

After getting in touch with an ecologist friend who was working in the Tanami at the time, I was pointed to a section of desert that had a high density of *L. kintorei* burrow systems. Once there it was just a matter of wandering around during the heat of the day, choosing the burrows that looked most active and returning just before dusk. It took a few hours of slowly walking around until finally, just as the sun was setting and the temperature dropped below that 30°C, I saw a flicker of movement among the Spinifex that was too large to be a Central Military Dragon (*Ctenophorus isolepis*). Peeking my head around a termite mound, I was ecstatic to see a large Great Desert Skink – measuring more than 30cm – staring back at me. After getting a couple of quick photos before the sun fully disappeared the lizard scampered off in search of food and I started the long walk back to the car feeling immensely pleased. This increased more so when I saw another individual cruising through the spinifex during my walk back.

PHOTOGRAPHIC EQUIPMENT USED

Canon 7D Mark II, Tokina 11–16mm, Twin Flash Canon EX 480, f14, 1/200s, ISO 400, 12mm. Edited in Lightroom.

SPECIES

Chillagoe Litter-skink (*Lygisaurus rococo*)

PHOTOGRAPHER

Peter Soltys

STATUS

LOCATION

Chillagoe, Queensland

NOTES

Snout-vent length 3.9cm. Listed as Near Threatened under the Queensland Nature Conservation Act. Occurs only in Chillagoe-Mungana National Park and Undara National Park. It is reported that these are both well managed and the species' habitat is buffered by the surrounding savanna woodland. There are no species-specific conservation measures in place at this time according to a report on the IUCN Red List website.

STORY BEHIND THE PHOTO

It was almost end of the summer 2018 when I received message from my colleague from north Queensland. "Hey Peter, do you want to go and look for *rococo*?"

And I was like: "roco-what?"

After some quick research I knew that I could not let this opportunity pass. I was thinking, what if I leave it for later and get hit by a car in the meantime and I'm not able to see it? No way! So, a few days after I was on the way to Cairns. After about a three-hour drive, we reached Chillagoe. This magical place is home to only about 190 people and is known for its Chillagoe burgers. If you are passing by you should definitely try it.

We managed to reach the appropriate rock formation after about an hour of searching. If I remember correctly, we saw only one *rococo* that day. Those things are pretty tiny, fast and hard to photograph, so I could not mess this up. I had only a couple of shots before the skinks disappeared again. It sat on a dry leaf and I managed to focus and fire off a couple of shots, and before I realised it, it was gone. I was worried that I had missed the shot as everything was in a rush, but once I checked the camera I could not believe how cool it colours were. To this day, *rococo* still is one of my favourite skinks.

PHOTOGRAPHIC EQUIPMENT USED

Canon EOS 5D mark IV, Canon EF 100mm f2.8 Macro USM, Canon Speedlight 600EX, combination of softbox and second diffusion, f22, 1/200s, ISO 400, flash Setting – ETTL. Editing using Lightroom Classic.

SPECIES

McCann's Skink (*Oligosoma maccanni*)

PHOTOGRAPHER

Tony Jewell

STATUS

EX   EW   CR   EN   VU   NT   **LC**

LOCATION

Origin of specimen: Danseys Pass, near Ranfurly, South Island

NOTES

Snout-vent length 6.5cm. Produces live young – an adaptation of lizards that are endemic to cool climatic regions of the world. Females are annual spring-summer breeders with an incubation period of 4–5 months.

STORY BEHIND THE PHOTO

McCann's Skink is easily pigeon-holed in the 'uninteresting common species' basket because it is abundant across large portions of its range in southern New Zealand. Indeed, across the driest parts of the island it is by far the most commonly encountered lizard, yet this familiarity masks the rightful status of McCann's as easily one of New Zealand's most extraordinary skink species. The altitudinal range achieved by this skink, from the coast to nearly 2km up in the mountains, reveals a remarkable adaptability. As well occurring in sand dunes and urban gardens, it can be found in lowland frost basins where winter temperatures can fall below -20°C, and on bare stony mountain crests so harsh that few plants can grow and snow may sit for more than half of the year. It also thrives in locations too hot and dry for any other local species, and changes its colour pattern across its range to suit localised niches shifting between rocky or grassy microhabitats. They can be beautiful little lizards too.

This photograph was taken at a time when I was actively expanding my knowledge of photographic techniques, before I had become set in my habits, and was undertaken as an exercise to try some of the ideas I had been thinking about. I was hoping to capture a scene with an adult pair sun-basking side-by-side, as is occasionally seen on sunny mornings, and found a pair sharing a rock in a montane gully near Ranfurly in the southern South Island. To set up the photo shoot, which would require co-operation from two specimens at once, I attempted to cool them down by placing them in a damp holding bag which was stashed for ten minutes or so in a cool dark cavity in a stream bank. While the skinks waited in this fashion I searched around for a prop that would allow for the critical combination of: 1. A good angle and background for the photo; and 2. A dearth of crevices or dense vegetation into which the skinks could vanish if they did decide to flee. The skinks were then positioned, the heavily gravid female in front and the male behind, and with only a little persuasion they came to hold their ground in a nice natural-looking pose, at which point I was able to begin taking a series of shots. I normally shoot with a wide focal depth as I tend to dislike images where half the subject is out of focus, but in this case there is an especially large span of distance between foreground and background, with the main subject matter in between. So I found from a series of different angles and focal depths attempted, a narrow depth of field was essential to help make the skinks pop out from potentially distracting surroundings. Even having the second skink in focus with the first just didn't work.

PHOTOGRAPHIC EQUIPMENT USED

Canon 400D, 900mm Tamron macro lens. Settings used not recorded, but natural lighting (no flash) and relatively low f-stop, perhaps between 4–8.

SPECIES

Southern Wet Tropics Shadeskink (*Saproscincus basiliscus*)

PHOTOGRAPHER

Shane Black

STATUS

 LC

LOCATION

Daintree National Park, far north Queensland

NOTES

Snout-vent length 4.9cm. Individuals sleep about 50cm above the ground on top of a leaf – a habit that keeps the skink out of the way of predators such as the Cane Toad, which frequents this species' range.

STORY BEHIND THE PHOTO

Most of my photography is centred around large venomous snakes, but in the 2015 wet season, with a shortage of elapids to photograph around home I started to look towards some of the less conspicuous species that share my local area. I'm talking about the small lizards and frogs that are often overlooked by not only myself, but many other photographers.

In 2015 I was living at Cooya Beach, in far north Queensland, which happens to be right next door to the Daintree National Park. I grabbed my camera gear and headed off there despite rainforest not being my most favoured habitat to herp in. As I was waiting for the Daintree River car ferry to come across, I could see it was raining quite heavily where I was heading. I was unperturbed as I hadn't done any photography for a few weeks due to the weather, and I was itching to get into it.

Once over the river I headed into the park, heading north towards Cape Tribulation. I decided to try a walking trail I knew of that bordered a creek and also went through some mangroves. The rain had temporarily stopped and I was keen to find something quickly to take advantage of the break in the weather. I hadn't been walking long when I started to see some small brown skinks scurrying through the leaf litter. They were Southern Wet Tropics Shadeskinks, which I had never photographed before. The first one had lost its tail, and the second was a juvenile with drab colouring, so I took my chances and pressed on hoping for a better-looking individual.

This time my patience paid off. Minutes later I spied a small flash of colour amid the wet dark forest floor. This fella was the one. Gently, I got on my stomach on the muddy ground, mozzies buzzing around my ears, and slowly approached him. To my delight he showed little fear and was actually quite inquisitive with me. Due to the very poor light in the dark rainforest and the weather, I needed to utilise my flashes for this shoot. I was pleased after I snapped the first pic that the dual speedlights didn't send him running off for cover. I quickly snapped off a couple more before he moved a short distance and stopped again.

I moved into a different position and got a couple of shots from a different angle before I decided enough was enough. Getting up soaking wet and covered in mud, I took a quick look on my camera of a few images. I was really happy how the flash showed off his colours, and because he was so bold it allowed me to get very close and really show this lizard's personality to the fullest. Macro photography of these little gems gives people a chance to appreciate them when they would otherwise take little notice.

PHOTOGRAPHIC EQUIPMENT USED

Nikon D800, Nikkor 105mm macro lens with dual speedlights on a Manfrotto bracket, f25, 1/250s, ISO 100. No photo editing software.

SPECIES

Weasel Skink (*Saproscincus mustelinus*)

PHOTOGRAPHER

Benjamin Stubbs

STATUS

EX   EW   CR   EN   VU   NT   **LC**

LOCATION

Craigieburn, Victoria

NOTES

Snout-vent length 5.5cm. The 'shadeskink' family, genus *Saproscincus*, contains 12 species distributed along Australia's east coast from Queensland to Victoria. As the name suggests, they are all shade loving, and are rarely found far from cover or seen basking in direct sun. Unlike most small lizards, Weasel Skinks are notably slow moving and appear surprisingly relaxed around people.

STORY BEHIND THE PHOTO

During early spring in September 2018, in what could be considered a bit of a wasteland along one of the local waterways in the northern suburbs of Melbourne, I ventured into the spread of debris hoping to locate some reptiles under the rubbish.

After walking through the majority of the area with no major success, I decided that I would focus my attention onto the skinks, the only reptiles I had seen so far that day, watching various Garden Skinks (*Lampropholis delicata*), Southern Water Skinks (*Eulamprus tympanum*) and large numbers of these fabulous little Weasel Skinks evade me as I wandered through the area.

This particular Weasel Skink was found under an old discarded wooden door. Luckily for me, it did not immediately evade me and shoot off into the surrounding shrubs. After it had scuttled out into the open from under the door, I managed to slowly lower myself onto the ground without it darting off. I find skinks to be challenging to photograph up close due to their readiness to quickly disappear into any cover nearby, never to be seen again.

This particular skink spent a good three or four minutes sitting within a couple feet of me while I took its photo, only finally moving off to cover once I stood up, being happy with the images I had captured.

Unknown to me at the time was the fact that a large number of discarded spikes from introduced prickly pears were scattered over the entire area, and thanks to my enthusiasm to photograph this cute little guy, they now covered most of my arms, hands and legs, although this just added to the memorable experience.

I think the beauty and personality of the majority of our small skink species are overlooked, with most people ignoring these little guys and missing the opportunity to see the amazing intricacies that can be seen on species such as this Weasel Skink.

PHOTOGRAPHIC EQUIPMENT USED

Nikon D7500, Tamron 90mm macro f/2.8, Nikon Sb-700 speedlight through 40cm soft box. Minor lighting adjustments made in Adobe Lightroom.

SPECIES

Shingleback (*Tiliqua rugosa aspera*)

PHOTOGRAPHER

Scott Eipper

STATUS

EX EW CR EN VU NT **LC**

LOCATION

Quilpe, Queensland

NOTES

Snout-vent length 31cm. Another of Australia's most recognisable species, found across much of the country. A study of 110 male-female partnerships in this species recorded many relationships lasting for more than 10 years and 31 lasting for more than 15 years. One relationship lasted for 27 years and continued beyond the end of the experiment. For long periods during the warmer months the partners remain by one another's side, never straying more than 30cm apart.

STORY BEHIND THE PHOTO

We had been driving through the hot western Queensland sun down a dusty track when we spied through the Mulga the glint of rusty iron in the scrub. There were a few old cars and a few rusted and flattened 44-gallon drums when I saw a pair Shinglebacks, with the male following the female intently.

Shingleback pairs meet up year after year to mate with the same partner – well usually anyway. I already had my camera out and was busy wandering along in front of them getting photos of the male following her, when she decided to stop in front of the old car body. Perfect. I laid down in the dust while I waved my hat to get her to look up, resulting in this image. The shade with fill flash really made the foreground pop, while the rusty car body gave a sense of history and a feel of Australiana.

PHOTOGRAPHIC EQUIPMENT USED

Nikon D300, Nikkor 18–77 mm telephoto, three Nikon SB800 flashes (one camera mounted, two mounted to a Manfrotto twin flash bracket), f16, 1/250s, ISO 200, +.7 exposure bias.

SPECIES

Burns' Dragon (*Amphibolurus burnsi*)

PHOTOGRAPHER

Gary Stephenson

STATUS

EX   EW   CR   EN   VU   NT   **LC**

LOCATION

Bladensburg National Park, Winton, Queensland

NOTES

Snout-vent length 13.5cm. Formerly treated as a northern population of Jacky Lizard (*A. muricatus*) until formally described as a separate species in 1985. Medium-sized agamid that inhabits semi-arid woodlands. A prolific breeder in captivity, with some females laying up to 15 eggs in a clutch and multiple clutches per season. Can be highly sexually dimorphic, with males having larger bulkier heads and bodies compared to females.

STORY BEHIND THE PHOTO

February 2012 had seen the tropical monsoon head south and it was now raining in western Queensland down into the 'Channel Country', an event that occurs on average every five to seven years. With plenty of rain about, some localised flooding and daytime temperatures in the mid-thirties, conditions were perfect for finding those often difficult to locate species in what is usually a very hostile environment – with temperatures often ten degrees hotter and windy.

Making the most of this opportunity, we headed west to Longreach, across the Thomson River and then north to tributaries that supply the mighty Cooper Creek. All this rainwater will eventually find its way into Kati Thanda–Lake Eyre, South Australia, when an all too infrequent boom period commences that can last for up to 12 months.

Upon arriving in Bladensburg National Park early in the afternoon, we slowly drove one of the many dirt roads when we located this heavily gravid Burns' Dragon basking on a fallen branch approximately 1.4m above the ground. Some dragons and monitor lizards found along roadside verges can be tolerant of an approaching vehicle, but when one attempts to exit the vehicle the lizard is usually quick to vanish. Conscious of the long grass immediately below and behind her, I decided to stay in the vehicle and wind down the window.

Once I secured the images I was after, I exited the vehicle to attempt a head shot. As fate would have it, she dropped to the ground and vanished into the long grass never to be seen of again.

The Burns' Dragon was not a target species on this trip as they are generally quite common around semi-permanent water courses in this area. However, the opportunity to shoot this image was too good to let pass given the scenic back drop that in drier times might just show grass stubble after being heavily grazed by kangaroos on a reddish-grey loamy soil.

It's probable that this might not have been her first clutch of eggs for the season with many egg-laying reptile species sometimes laying two or three times in optimal conditions such as this.

Two other very common agamid species were also observed in the immediate area, namely the Central Netted Dragon (*Ctenophorus nuchalis*) and the Central Bearded Dragon (*Pogona vitticeps*), and almost identical photographic techniques were used with these lizards, although these species are often seen on or just above the ground on graded rocks or on fallen timber.

PHOTOGRAPHIC EQUIPMENT USED

Nikon D300s, Sigma DG 120–400mm 4.5–5.6 APO HSM zoom lens at 200mm, f11, 1/500s, ISO 200, with heavy cloud cover. Processed in Photoshop CS2 with some image sharpening, light and saturation enhancement.

SPECIES

Frillneck (*Chlamydosaurus kingi*)

PHOTOGRAPHER

Gunther Schmida

STATUS

EX   EW   CR   EN   VU   NT   **LC**

LOCATION

Darwin, Northern Territory

NOTES

Snout-vent length 25.8cm. One of the world's most iconic animals. Rarely seen in dry season, when high in canopy. In wet season commonly seen on trees, 1–2m off ground. In spring breeding season male performs an elaborate dance to impress female; she signals her interest with a flurry of head bobs. Females dig a hole and lay 10–15 eggs, which hatch about 10 weeks later.

STORY BEHIND THE PHOTO

From a photographer's point of view, dragons are definitely my most favourite reptilian subject, and for good reason. While most reptiles prefer to lead cryptic lives, dragons are right out there, almost showing off.

After I touched down on Australian soil over 50 years ago, it was bearded dragons that I first set eyes on, but the dragon I really yearned for, the famous Frillneck, or Frilled Lizard, proved to be a much more difficult quarry to find.

Back then I worked in Gladstone in central coastal Queensland, and had no problem finding plenty of road-killed 'frillies', but finding a live one was a different matter. It took months before I finally got lucky and got my first shots, and these were quite ordinary by any standard.

Since those early days I have found countless frillies all over their range, usually on the sides of roads after some rain had fallen, and they had come down from the canopy to feed on the ground. Naturally I have taken many shots in that time. As frillies are almost always eager to display their well-known defensive pose with spread frill and wide open mouth, they are not afraid to have a go at anyone who gets too close for their liking, so it is relatively easy to get impressive shots.

However, Frillnecks don't just have an impressive defensive display, they can also walk and run on their hind legs only, and they do so quite often, only usually away from the photographer. Trying to get one to run at an angle towards me proved a tad more difficult, but was finally achieved with the help of my good friend and herpetologist, Dr Gavin Bedford, who was in the process of opening the largest reptile display in Darwin at the time. I can't remember how many times we tried but I got the shot sooner than expected – thanks Gavin.

Allowing for some distance to make panning the running lizard and holding frame and focus easier, I used the longest lens I had at the time, a 130–400mm zoom set at 300mm. I also did not try to frame the lizard too tight, as it is difficult enough to capture moving subjects at the best of times. Cropping the shot as required in an editing programme is the better option, than taking countless shots trying to get it right.

Although I prefer to focus most of my shots manually, autofocus came in very handy in this situation.

The shots were taken in the morning, but even so, as the November sun quickly moved high into the sky it soon became too hot for everyone, especially the lizards.

PHOTOGRAPHIC EQUIPMENT USED

Nikon D80 DSLR, Sigma 130–400mm zoom set at 300mm, f10, 1/1600s, ISO 400. Image cropped by about 40 per cent in Photoshop CS5.

SPECIES

Tawny Dragon (*Ctenophorus decresii*)

PHOTOGRAPHER

Steve Wilson

STATUS

EX EW CR EN VU NT **LC**

LOCATION

Telowie Gorge, South Australia

NOTES

Snout-vent length 7.5cm. Alternative name Tawny Crevice Dragon. Seeks shelter in crevices in rocky hills. Known for polymorphism in throat colour, which can range from grey and white to bright red.

STORY BEHIND THE PHOTO

It is a rare event during herpetological photography, to have the main subject 'photo-bombed', but this happened while I was stalking Tawny Dragons at Telowie Gorge. When the weather is good it is a great place to see plenty of lizards. Tawny Dragons are particularly abundant and obvious. They are rock inhabitants and most individuals select elevated perching sites on stones and boulders, often quite close to walking tracks. This makes them ideal subjects for in situ photography. The fact that many of the males are brilliantly coloured certainly adds to their appeal.

It is also common to see Masked Rock Skinks (*Liopholis personata*) along the horizontal rock crevices. They generally sit with the head or forebody exposed, ready to ambush passing prey.

I spent an afternoon taking pictures of the Tawny Dragons, with mixed success. They spend extended periods in conspicuous poses on exposed sites but that does not mean they always cooperate with the photographer.

The concept of a warm dragon, its body angled into the sun, elevated high on a red rock with its orange face and blue and black flanks splashed against a blue sky makes an evocative image. But it is all over in an instant with one careless movement as I try to get that extra few steps around an obstructing shrub to make the possible picture a reality. That splendid image in my mind's eye is now reduced to just 'what might have been'.

I try to take a series of shots as I gradually close the gap. Snap a picture, take a step, snap another and inch a little closer. I was going through this process with an attractive male dragon that was only too aware of my presence and poised to flee.

As I gradually closed the gap, taking pictures, an interloper walked through the set. Luckily I had the camera to my eye focussed on the dragon during the few seconds that a Masked Rock Skink stepped into the frame. It did not pause and it did not rush. It simply ambled through, allowing me time for just one shot.

Skink and dragon paid each other no attention. Why should they? Neither predator nor prey, they are simply residents sharing space and resources in the same rocky habitat. Like those neighbours who are no problem at all but with whom you really have nothing in common. But the brief moment their trajectories intersected meant something to me as I was there to capture it.

PHOTOGRAPHIC EQUIPMENT USED

Canon EOS 30D with 300 mm lens and 1.4x converter, f9, 1/400s, ISO 100.

SPECIES

Central Netted Dragon (*Ctenophorus nuchalis*)

PHOTOGRAPHER

Ken Griffiths

STATUS

EX   EW   CR   EN   VU   NT   LC

LOCATION

Gundabooka National Park, New South Wales

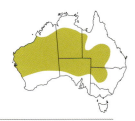

NOTES

Snout-vent length 11.5cm. One of the most common and widespread lizards in the arid parts of Australia. Often seen basking in an elevated position monitoring their territory. This has proven to be a suitable and popular species in captivity.

STORY BEHIND THE PHOTO

This photograph was taken as part of a field survey with the Australian Herpetological Society in October 2018 at Gundabooka. Gundabooka National Park and SCA is a vast area covering some 64,000ha of country that is rich in Aboriginal heritage and wildlife and lies about an hour's drive to the west of Bourke, New South Wales.

A lot of the searching for reptiles is done driving the minor roads and service trails that are in the park. There is not a lot of material to lift or turn in this sort of country so driving is a comfortable and time-effective way to look for wildlife both day and night. Central Netted Dragons are one of the most common reptile species seen during the surveys. They are often found basking on a rock or log by the roadside. When they warm up they have striking patterns and colours, which make them one of the most enjoyable reptiles to photograph.

PHOTOGRAPHIC EQUIPMENT USED

Canon 6D Mark II, 100mm f2.8L macro lens, natural light, f11, 1/500s, ISO 320. Sharpening and minor levels adjusted in Adobe Photoshop CS6.

SPECIES

Slater's Ring-tailed Dragon (*Ctenophorus slateri*)

PHOTOGRAPHER

Jules Farquhar

STATUS

EX EW CR EN VU NT **LC**

LOCATION

Wolfe Creek Crater, Western Australia

NOTES

Snout-vent length 9.1cm. Widespread through the arid interior of northern Australia. Likely plays an important role in arid ecosystems as a prey source for many higher-order predators. A prolific breeder when conditions are favourable.

STORY BEHIND THE PHOTO

About 300,000 years ago a meteorite punched a massive hole into the Australian outback, pulverizing the underlying earth to form a rocky crater rim in an otherwise featureless desert landscape. And on 10 September 2018, we drove 140km south of Halls Creek to look for reptiles at this geological wonder – the Wolfe Creek Meteorite Crater. We had just spent the past ten days driving around the Kimberley Region of Western Australia, collecting data on some of the region's lesser known reptile species. Wolfe Creek Crater is on the southern margin of the Kimberley, where red sand dunes start to predominate in the landscape.

It was the late dry season and we were fairly far inland, so the humidity was much more bearable compared to Darwin where the trip began. As well as other species we hoped to see Slater's Ring-tailed Dragons at the crater, where they are abundant on the broken quartzite rock slabs of its outer slopes. When we arrived at the base of the crater, I grabbed my camera and began walking up the slope to search for these dragons. It quickly became apparent that they were everywhere and that, because of the ever-present tourists, these lizards had become accustomed to people walking around them. I spent about 40 minutes walking up and down the slope taking pictures and scanning the rocks with my binoculars for more lizard heads.

At 3pm I saw a large adult dragon perched on a rock in the shade of a tree, and slowly approached it. This lizard was so bold that I could get within 30cm of it and take this picture as it looked around with complete indifference. Because it was a sunny day, there was no need for flashes to light the subject. However, most of this lizard's body was in the shade while the spinifex hummock in the background was in full sunlight. It is generally not ideal for photography to have such contrasting lighting, because the camera can only expose for one or the other. With my flashes all the way back at the car, I decided to just use a wide aperture to allow enough light into the camera to properly expose for the shaded lizard. This meant that the sky and sunlit spinifex in the background were slightly overexposed, but I knew I could simply reduce these highlights in post editing.

PHOTOGRAPHIC EQUIPMENT USED

Canon EOS 5D Mark IV, Canon EF 100mm f/2.8L IS USM macro lens, f6.3, 1/250s, ISO 250, RAW. Minor adjustments to exposure using Adobe Lightroom.

SPECIES

Swamplands Lashtail (*Tropicagma temporalis*)

PHOTOGRAPHER

Benjamin Stubbs

STATUS

EX   EW   CR   EN   VU   NT   **LC**

LOCATION

Fogg Dam, Northern Territory

NOTES

Snout-vent length 10.9cm. Most commonly found in trees close to water. Often called the 'Ta ta lizard' as they have a habit of waving their arms. Also found in New Guinea and Indonesia.

STORY BEHIND THE PHOTO

During a trip to Darwin in January 2018 I found myself at Fogg Dam a few times, and on this particular occasion I was on the hunt for birds to photograph, but with little rainfall the pickings were slim. It was late in the morning and there was little to no activity of any sort, from either reptiles or birds.

Every time I am lucky enough to travel up to the Northern Territory in and around Darwin I always see these beautiful lizards on the move, and although they are numerous, I always crack a smile when I see them scurrying away in that all-too-familiar dragon fashion.

Because they are so commonly seen they are not an animal that I photograph very often, but this particular individual captured my attention as it moved away from me in the Fogg Dam car park and perched so beautifully upon this branch.

These opportunistic photographs can sometimes end up being my favourites, and the symmetry created by this lizard's tail and the branch was a very pleasing result.

I was lucky enough that this little guy had its body angled towards me and the sun was at a nice angle, but as always I did not have a large amount of time to photograph this animal, as it made off down the embankment soon after this photo was taken.

PHOTOGRAPHIC EQUIPMENT USED

Nikon D7500, Nikkor 200–500mm VR. Minor lighting adjustments made in Adobe Lightroom.

SPECIES

Boyd's Forest Dragon (*Lophosaurus boydii*)

PHOTOGRAPHER

Michael Cermak

STATUS

EX   EW   CR   EN   VU   NT   **LC**

LOCATION

Cape Tribulation, north Queensland

NOTES

Snout-vent length 15cm. Synonymous with far north Queensland and regarded by many as one of Australia's most impressive rainforest inhabitants. This arboreal species can often be seen clinging to tree trunks about 2m off the ground. Adults are instantly recognisable through the prominent crest on their head, which give them a truly prehistoric appearance.

STORY BEHIND THE PHOTO

Confined to the wet tropics of North Queensland, the Boyd's Forest Dragon is not only spectacular-looking lizard, but one with fascinating ecology as well. Jordie Torr has done his PhD on this species and shed some light on the lizard's behavioural dynamics and cryptic habits.

I saw my first Boyd's in 1972, at Cooya Beach near Mossman. It wasn't in the rainforest, but in one of Brian Barnett's cages. I was blown away by this spectacular agamid and I couldn't wait to see one in its natural habitat. In those days, tourism in north Queensland was almost non-existent and the locals rarely ventured into the wilderness. What's more, rural landowners didn't mind us herpers entering onto their properties in pursuit of reptiles – all of that has changed since. Also, national parks were fewer than today, so collecting in places like the Mossman Gorge was a regular activity and that's where I found my first wild Boyd's. I didn't own a camera in those days, so it was many years later when I started photographing this saurian gem both in the wild and in captivity.

Whilst working at Cape Tribulation in the mid-2000s, I saw many Boyd's along the board walks, usually sitting tight against tree trunks in the daytime, turning around the trunk to get out of sight when approached. I was looking for a different shot from the norm, with a different angle, but it wasn't easy to find in situ what I was looking for, so I arranged this Boyd's on a rock on an elevated bank and took a few shots from slightly below the animal's head. Boyd's are easy to work with, and when put in the desired position they usually prop up and stay still. This was one of my last photo sessions with a film camera before I bought my first digital, the Canon 20D.

PHOTOGRAPHIC EQUIPMENT USED

Canon EOS 1v, 28–70mm L 2.8 lens, two Canon Speedlites 550EX flashguns, Fuji Velvia, f22, 1/60s, ISO 50.

SPECIES

Eastern Water Dragon (*Intellagama lesueurii lesueurii*)

PHOTOGRAPHER

Gunther Schmida

STATUS

EX EW CR EN VU NT **LC**

LOCATION

Forest Lake, Brisbane, Queensland

NOTES

Snout-vent length 24.5cm. This species, perhaps more than any other, has adapted to and thrives around humans. They are a common sight in parks and gardens within their range. Recent work by Australian scientists has shown that this species has responded to urbanisation in a number of physical and behavioural ways. Continued research has also shown that they have much more complex social interactions than first thought. Unfortunately, while studying this species researchers in Queensland detected an outbreak of a potentially fatal fungal disease which may be an emerging threat for this and other dragon species.

STORY BEHIND THE PHOTO

Probably the most urbanised of all large Australian lizards, water dragons are truly fantastic creatures. Extremely shy in the wild, where they are just about impossible to get close enough to for an half decent shot, even when using a super-long lens, they behave just the opposite in human environments.

Wherever there is a park in eastern Australia with some water and cover about, water dragons are present and often in large numbers. They eat just about everything, even pellets used by people to feed other wildlife.

It is very easy to get close, sometimes close enough to take a portrait with a standard lens. Even so, to get an impressive image the light must be right.

I prefer natural soft light provided by the sun on bright days with thin high cloud cover when photographing all dragons in situ, simply because the shadows are softer in diffused light. I also use my long tele-zoom to give me a better perspective. I never use fill flash because, in my opinion, it gives the shots an unrealistic appearance. Instead I use reflectors if needed.

This beautiful large male was captured on one such spring day in Forest Lake, a Brisbane suburb with a nice park and plenty of water, and a large population of friendly water dragons. He was the dominant male with a harem of several females and juveniles in this area of the park, with a few smaller subordinate males hanging around in the vicinity. There were many other groups of dragons elsewhere.

Although the dragons were as used to people as they could possibly be, I still moved very slowly when approaching this male, to make sure it stayed in the position I wanted to photograph it in. That is why I had set my 120–400mm zoom at 400mm as I moved in and slowly shortened it to 300mm, when I was happy with the framing of the shot before taking it. All my shots are taken hand-held.

PHOTOGRAPHIC EQUIPMENT USED

Nikon D300 DSLR, Sigma APO zoom 120/400mm set on 300mm, f9, 1/1600s, ISO 400. Image cropped by about 20 per cent in Photoshop CS5.

SPECIES

Thorny Devil (*Moloch horridus*)

PHOTOGRAPHER

Ross McGibbon

STATUS

EX EW CR EN VU NT **LC**

LOCATION

Eurardy Region, Western Australia

NOTES

Snout-vent length 11cm. An iconic species unlike any other. A specialised feeder that eats only small black ants. They stand beside a trail and pick off up to 5,000 in one sitting.

STORY BEHIND THE PHOTO

As a boy, I used to read about the iconic Australian Thorny Devil in books and dream of seeing them in the wild one day. When I relocated from Queensland to Western Australia in 2016, I couldn't wait to explore Western Australia and search for all the reptiles I didn't have access to on the east coast. Needless to say, the Thorny Devil was at the top of my list. At the beginning of 2017 I began planning a six-week road trip from Perth to Darwin for March and April. Over the course of the trip I covered 16,000km and photographed around 60 reptile species. I was ecstatic to start the trip with this Thorny Devil.

Thorny Devils are very tolerant of high outback temperatures and they are capable of basking in the sun during the hottest parts of the day. With this in mind, I was keeping a keen eye on the road as the day warmed up. At 2pm I was roughly 600km north of Perth and the temperature was hovering around 35°C. I whizzed passed a Thorny Devil basking in the middle of the road and performed one of the quickest U-turns of my life. I safely removed it from the busy highway and took a series of photos.

Beginning with a wide-angle lens, I was having trouble photographing the lizard in direct sunlight. The sun was causing harsh shadows and I was losing some of the detail. Rather than persist in this manner, I switched to my macro lens. I also wanted to capture elements of the sun, and achieved this by orienting my shot so the sun's rays highlighted the margins of the devil's spines. With the sun now behind the lizard I utilised an external flash to fill in the side of the animal that was now in shadow. The result was a nicely lit portrait with the background blurred enough to ensure the viewer's focus remains on the Thorny Devil.

The tilt of the head, together with the downward curvature of the mouth and squint of the eye gives the impression that the lizard is quite suspicious of me. Real or imagined, the expression makes you wonder what's going on in the mind of the animal during such an encounter.

PHOTOGRAPHIC EQUIPMENT USED

Canon 700D, Canon 60mm macro lens, external speedlight flash and diffuser. Post processing using Adobe Lightroom.

SPECIES

Dwarf Bearded Dragon (*Pogona minor*)

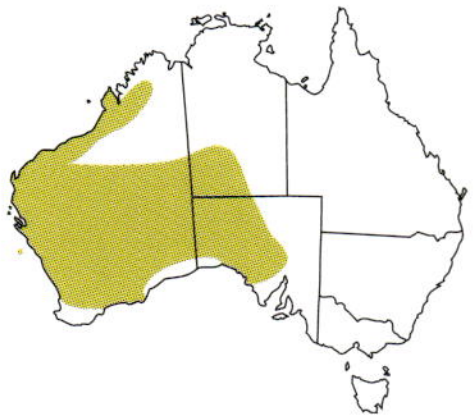

PHOTOGRAPHER

Jari Cornelis

STATUS

EX EW CR EN VU NT **LC**

LOCATION

Ilkurlka, Western Australia

NOTES

Snout-vent length up to 16.3cm. Varies in size depending on location – one gravid female measured a snout-vent length of only 8.9cm. Semi-arboreal and occupies a wide variety of habitats, including eucalypt forest, coastal dunes, heathlands, open woodlands and arid regions populated with spinifex. Also comfortable in small pockets of natural habitat around urban areas within their range. Typically lays around eight eggs.

STORY BEHIND THE PHOTO

I captured this image on 14 January 2019, close to the most remote roadhouse in the world. After almost two months on the road I was in the middle of the most taxing part of the trip. At this stage I was travelling with my mate Elliot through the Great Victoria Desert on the hunt for the legendary Western Desert Taipan. Unfortunately, we were unsuccessful after days of searching with barely any rest except for in the hottest part of the day because nothing could bare the 48°C heat and neither could we. We found many other species of animals while driving up and down dunes and corrugation, including this Dwarf Bearded Dragon that was still a bit groggy and clinging to a branch in the early morning before the sun's heat had hit.

An extremely intense fire had recently raged through the area burning everything to a crisp causing an evacuation of the roadhouse as the fire reached their doorstep. Broken down cars that were consumed by the fire had dried pools of metal coming out from under them which were the melted engine blocks. Despite all the chaos that had occurred recently, this resilient lizard was able to survive in this wasteland and was the only vertebrate besides birds that we saw in this section of the aftermath, which was also the worst part of the burn that we saw.

Once we began photographing the sun was up and pummelling our backs and we could only spend a few minutes of taking pictures. We had spent too much time discussing and questioning how this lizard was even able to live out here, but we both got photos that we liked. I guess the scenery offered us a unique opportunity and any animal would have looked good with this background.

PHOTOGRAPHIC EQUIPMENT USED

Canon 700D with EF-S 10–18mm f/4.5-5.6 IS STM. Lightroom used for post-processing.

SPECIES

Central Bearded Dragon (*Pogona vitticeps*)

PHOTOGRAPHER

Jari Cornelis

STATUS

EX   EW   CR   EN   VU   NT   **LC**

LOCATION

Tobermorey Station, Northern Territory

NOTES

Snout-vent length 25cm. Until recently this species was restricted to Australia's arid interior. It is now probably the most widely kept pet lizard in the world, due to its striking appearance and calm temperament. They are also easy to breed and produce about 25 eggs on average, although clutches of up to 50 eggs have been recorded. Strangely the related Eastern Bearded Dragon (*P. barbata*) doesn't fair nearly so well in captivity, although to the untrained eye the two species look remarkably similar.

STORY BEHIND THE PHOTO

This photo was taken on 20 November 2018. This was at the very start of the biggest road trip I had ever undertaken; at the time I was travelling with my girlfriend as I switched travel companions a few times along the journey. Aleesha and I had just crossed the border from Queensland into the Northern Territory.

As we pulled off the road to take a selfie, I saw a medium-sized lizard dart across the road and into the scrub. After a few minutes of searching I found it to be a Central Bearded Dragon, the first new species of the trip for me so I was extremely excited. We had spent a few days driving through Queensland dodging bad weather and not seeing many animals, so it was a relief to only just make it over the border and find an animal neither of us had seen before and what a beautiful specimen at that.

I started photographing him with a lens I had only just bought so I was still a bit unfamiliar with the settings required to capture the subject with nice lighting while still allowing enough natural light in to see the background. Lucky for me a massive storm was rolling in, so the background looked interesting, but it took a few attempts to be able to see it in the photos. Just as I had it figured out the wind started to pick up and I could feel the storm was closing in on us so the image shown above was the last photo I took before leaving the animal and retreating to our car to find our way to Tobermorey Station where we still had to set up our tent before the storm hit.

PHOTOGRAPHIC EQUIPMENT USED

Canon 700D with EF-S 10–18mm f/4.5–5.6 IS STM. Lightroom was used for post-processing.

SPECIES

Smooth-snouted Earless Dragon (*Tympanocryptis intima*)

PHOTOGRAPHER

Steve Wilson

STATUS

EX EW CR EN VU NT **LC**

LOCATION

Mitchell Grass Downs, Queensland

NOTES

Snout-vent length 6.1cm. About eight eggs per clutch. Members of this genus lack the external ear opening common to all other lizards. Arid members of this genus are of little conservation concern, but grassland specialists along the east coast of Australia are some of the most imperilled reptiles in the country due to land clearing and landscape changes resulting from agriculture. One such species was only formally described in mid-2019 and may already be extinct, making it the first reptile to be considered formally extinct on the Australian mainland.

STORY BEHIND THE PHOTO

When I encountered this juvenile Smooth-snouted Earless Dragon behaving in a way that defied both thermal tolerance and logic, I could not resist recording the scene.

December is a challenging time to visit Queensland's Mitchell Grass Downs bioregion. When I joined friends on a reptile photographing trip for a week through Longreach, Winton and Richmond, the maximum temperature reached 42°C or higher every day.

There had been some good rains previously, triggering plenty of reptile activity outside the heat window, in the early morning, late afternoon and at night. With herpetological exploration out of the question during the day, we took time off, mindful of our own thermal management issues.

Air conditioned venues were popular, particularly those that also catered to our particular interests in the region's Cretaceous heritage. The Lark Quarry Dinosaur Trackways, Kronosaurus Corner and The Age of Dinosaurs were cool magnets for a gaggle of hot herpetologists.

It was in the car park at The Age of Dinosaurs that we chanced upon the tiny earless dragon. In 42°C this misguided juvenile, with a snout-vent length of about 3cm, was perched in full sun. Official measurements are taken in the shade, so the mind boggles as to what temperature it was actually subjecting itself to. And to compound the little lizard's endurance, it had selected a black metal chain atop a bollard as a perching site.

I chose a couple of photo angles to record the scenario. By crouching low I could include a horizon with blue sky. When I stood a little higher, with a low f-stop to reduce any distracting background clutter, I achieved a neutral, diffuse backdrop of the natural reddish substrate. That is the angle I think worked best because the image needs the uniformly warm colours that reflect the conditions of the day. The angle also helps because the backdrop is visible beneath the dragon, highlighting the posture it has selected. Its body is raised high on skinny legs and its tail is in minimal point contact for stability as it perches on the searing hot metal. And in spite of this, as I indulge in a little anthropomorphising, the lizard retains a facial expression of beatific calm!

The photo poses a couple of questions. How could such a tiny lizard, barely larger than the first joint of my little finger, tolerate such extreme temperatures? Blasted by intense sunshine from above and radiant heat from below, it appears to have selected intolerable conditions that one would expect to be lethal. The other question of course, when there are plenty of shady shrubs around, is: Why?

PHOTOGRAPHIC EQUIPMENT USED

Canon EOS 6D with 100 mm lens, f5, 1/2500s, ISO 200.

SPECIES

Spiny-tailed Monitor (*Varanus acanthurus*)

PHOTOGRAPHER

Steve Swanson

STATUS

EX EW CR EN VU NT **LC**

LOCATION

Mount Isa, Queensland

NOTES

Total length 63cm. Predominantly terrestrial. Unlike many similar-sized monitors, this species lives mainly under rocks or boulders, or in crevices. They are often found in these locations during the day, suggesting that they aren't as active as foragers compared to other monitors. Feed largely on insects and small lizards, and like most ambush predators they tend to eat anything wandering past that they can overpower. Popular in captivity and now the most widely kept species of small monitor around the world. Clutch size normally up to 18 eggs. The young hatch after three to five months and measure around 15cm.

STORY BEHIND THE PHOTO

The Mount Isa region of north-western Queensland is a hot-spot of reptile diversity, and I was fortunate enough to live there for about 18 months in 2008–09. Spiny-tailed Monitors occur across a large part of northern and central Australia and are common in the Mount Isa area. They usually shelter in a rock crevice, or on the open plains, in a burrow beneath a rock or fallen termite mound.

One February morning in 2009, while we were driving between Mount Isa and Dajarra, my wife spotted this magnificent specimen – by far the most attractive I have encountered – basking on a termite mound by the side of the road.

PHOTOGRAPHIC EQUIPMENT USED

Pentax K10D with Sigma 18–50mm, f11, 1/250s, full sunlight. Some minor adjustments to the image using Photoshop.

SPECIES

Perentie (*Varanus giganteus*)

PHOTOGRAPHER

Ross McGibbon

STATUS

EX   EW   CR   EN   VU   NT   **LC**

LOCATION

Gnarloo Station, Western Australia

NOTES

Total length 2.4m. Australia's largest monitor and the fourth-largest living lizard on Earth, after the Komodo Dragon, Asian Water Monitor and Crocodile Monitor. Active by day and known to forage over an area of several square kilometres.

STORY BEHIND THE PHOTO

It's late afternoon on a sunny winter's day in June and my friends and I are heading back from a surfing break north of Carnarvon, Western Australia. Up ahead on the track we spot a large 2m male Perentie monitor feeding on a smaller road-kill Perentie on the side of the road. As I exit the car and approach for a closer look, the massive monitor decides it wants to escape in the direction I am approaching from. It lunges at me in order to put me on the back foot so it can scoot around, then takes off at full speed towards some coastal cliffs around 100m away.

I pursue it and eventually catch up, but am too eager and get a little close. The Perentie recoils its tail and unleashes it across my lower legs. I liken the experience to a fully-grown man whipping me across the legs with an extension cord as hard as he can. I look down and notice a large blood blister immediately forming on my inner calf muscle, but I am that excited to be in the presence of my first Perentie in the wild that I hardly notice the pain. That said, I learn my lesson and back off an extra foot or two. You would think I would remember the numerous lace monitors doing this to me around campsites in south-east Queensland as a kid, but 25 years on, I still can't help getting close.

The Perentie settles on the top of the cliff and lies on its belly on the warm rocks with its legs splayed out like a dog. It appears to be more relaxed in my presence now that it has shown me who's boss. I remain with it for the next 15 minutes while my friends offer to retrieve my camera from our campsite. When they return, they watch as I photograph it using a wide-angle lens. It's late in the afternoon and the sun is providing the perfect light to show the detail of the Perentie, as well as expose the ocean in the background. To achieve the composition I wanted, I crept to just out of tail striking range. I also needed the Perentie's head to face a certain way, so I used my hat as a distraction for a moment. With pinpoint precision, the Perentie whipped it out of my hand with its tail, sending it flying about 4m. This time I am pleased it only struck the hat and not my hand as well.

After a short while, I am happy with my photos and I return to the road to bring back his road-kill meal for him to enjoy as a thank you for being such a good subject, despite the initial love-tap across the legs.

PHOTOGRAPHIC EQUIPMENT USED

Canon 700D, Tamron 10–24mm wide-angle lens, external speedlight flash and diffuser. Post processing using Adobe Lightroom.

SPECIES

Sand Monitor (*Varanus gouldii gouldii*)

PHOTOGRAPHER

Jules Farquhar

STATUS

EX EW CR EN VU NT **LC**

LOCATION

Mutawintji National Park, New South Wales

NOTES

Total length 1.6m. Also known Gould's Monitor. An active species which covers great swathes of land in search of food. They are skilled diggers quite capable of making their own burrows. Feed on a wide variety of prey items, including highly venomous snakes that they come across and also roadkill. Lay their eggs in termite mounds, which help to incubate them and protect them from predators.

STORY BEHIND THE PHOTO

I left Victoria on 24 September 2017, with my rusty old Troop Carrier packed full of sardines and Weetbix. I brought a botanist friend along with me who was keen to see what herping was all about. We were headed for Nanya Research Station in outback New South Wales, where we would spend the next three weeks collecting data for herpetological research. We left two days ahead of schedule so that we could first take a detour to the remarkable rock formations of Mutawintji National Park to see Barrier Range Dragons, and some isolated populations of herpetofauna atypical of western New South Wales, such as the White's Skink and Black-headed Monitor. After only a day in Mutawintji we saw enough Barrier Range Dragons to last a lifetime, and had a fortuitous encounter with a Black-headed Monitor foraging in a gorge. On 26 September, we left Mutawintji and headed back towards Broken Hill. As to be expected from the outback in spring, the roads were crawling with Shinglebacks, Central Bearded Dragons, and Sand Monitors. In most cases we would pull over and move the Shinglebacks and dragons off the road to prevent a run-in with the next car. Sand Monitors, on the other hand, are quick and difficult to catch.

It was a sunny afternoon, at 4pm, when we saw a Sand Monitor basking in the middle of the road, about a 20-minute drive out of Mutawintji. I stopped the car 30m away from the lizard and did what any lizard fancier worth their salt would do – I grabbed my camera, jumped out of the car and proceeded to crawl along the ground towards the lizard at snail speed. At this point in time, I had already photographed Sand Monitors throughout much of Australia, but I was eager to try out my new telephoto lens. The lizard was cautious, and begun slowly walking towards some shrubs at the road's edge as I crept closer taking photos. I wanted to get a head-on photo of the lizard, which meant I needed to get behind the roadside shrubs to which the lizard was heading and wait for it to walk right towards me. Humans are not capable of serpentine locomotion, but since a good photo was at stake, I somehow managed to slither beneath the dense shrubs on my stomach while keeping the camera up off the sand. Once I was in position, I began taking photos as the lizard continued walking towards the shrubs, blissfully unaware that I was hiding within. The lizard stopped just before the shrubs, so I slowly crept out towards it and took this photograph from 3.5m away, which is the closest distance the camera lens could focus.

PHOTOGRAPHIC EQUIPMENT USED

Canon EOS 7D Mark II, Canon EF 400mm f/5.6L USM telephoto lens, f5.6, 1/4000s, ISO 500, RAW. Minor adjustments to exposure made using Adobe Lightroom.

SPECIES

Mangrove Monitor (*Varanus indicus*)

PHOTOGRAPHER

Gary Stephenson

STATUS

EX   EW   CR   EN   VU   NT   **LC**

LOCATION

Iron Range (Cape York Peninsula), Queensland

NOTES

Total length 1.2m. Range extends through northern Australia, New Guinea, the Solomon Islands and the Marshall Islands, as well as parts of South-East Asia. Within this distribution across thousands of miles and hundreds of islands, these lizards exhibit large variations in size, pattern and scalation.

STORY BEHIND THE PHOTO

No herpetological adventure in Australia is complete without a visit to the wet tropics, and specifically to the rainforests of the eastern Cape York Peninsula where the Holy Grail is to find a Green Python (*Morelia viridis*).

Iron Range (Kutini-Payamu) National Park has been a paradise for both professional and amateur herpetologists alike, but there are many other species that inhabit these northern rainforests besides Green Pythons, and these areas are yielding many new species, particularly frogs, geckos and skinks.

Only in the last few years has it been confirmed that two (possibly three) species of 'mangrove' monitor exist in these northern rainforests: the 'traditional' Mangrove Monitor (*Varanus indicus*) and Blue-tailed Monitor (*Varanus doreanus*).

I have personally located the Mangrove Monitor in the Northern Territory prior to the arrival of Cane Toads (*Rhinella marina*), but numbers have materially declined since their invasion. However I've not observed them in north Queensland and I'd heard rumours of the Blue-taileds occurring up there as well.

Cape York Peninsula is far more accessible than it used to be, with sealed roads ever encroaching towards the 'tip' and the formed dirt roads in reasonable order save for the corrugations that get progressively worse as the dry season comes to a close. It was in November 2014 that the race was on to get to Iron Range before the monsoon started. At 1,940km from Brisbane, it's a good three-day drive.

It was hot upon our arrival – in the mid-thirties – and the humidity was energy-sapping. That, along with the myriad of invertebrate life, including leeches, mosquitos, sand flies and the like, made for getting out and about both during the day and of a night very uncomfortable.

But we were here to work and in the morning the strategy was to hit the mangroves and then clumsily make our way back along the creek towards the rainforest as the sun rose higher in the sky. Other than numerous rainbow skinks (*Carlia* sp.), with the males in full breeding colours, there was not much else about. The end of the 'dry' can be a very uninspiring experience.

Not to be deterred, we ventured into the rainforest where we located this active subadult Mangrove Monitor. One of Australia's most attractive monitors, they are also noticeably far more relaxed compared with some other species, evidenced here by a casual flickering of the tongue.

PHOTOGRAPHIC EQUIPMENT USED

Nikon D300S, Nikkor 18–200mm 3.5–5.6 G ED zoom lens at 130mm, f18, 1/250s, ISO 200, camera mounted Nikon Speedlight SB-600 on manual setting at ½ power with a circular diffuser and one additional speedlight at ¼ power mounted approximately 45° to the right of the subject.

SPECIES

Mertens' Water Monitor (*Varanus mertensi*)

PHOTOGRAPHER

Lachlan Gilding

STATUS

EX   EW   CR   **EN**   VU   NT   LC

LOCATION

Prince Regent National Park, Western Australia

NOTES

Total length 1.1m. Since frogs make up a large part of this species' diet, it is unsurprising that the arrival of the introduced and toxic Cane Toad has caused its decline. There is evidence of rapid decline eight months after the arrival of Cane Toads in an area, and an overall decline in abundance by nearly 80 per cent was estimated between 2004–06.

STORY BEHIND THE PHOTO

The Mertens' Water Monitor can be a fairly common sight across the top end of Australia. This species can generally be found residing around creeks and streams, where it hunts on both land and under the water. Mertens' Water Monitors are one of several species that are known to become very bold around people, and this can happen either when an animal has prolonged exposure to humans or little to no exposure.

In October 2017, whilst on an expedition into Prince Regent National Park, I was walking a very remote creek line behind our camp when I noticed this very large female Mertens' Water Monitor basking on the opposite bank. After spotting the animal I waded into the waste deep water and used my 150–600 Sigma to start snapping a few photos. As I was taking the photos, instead of shying away from the camera the animal instead walked in my direction and entered the water with me. For the next 30 minutes this beautiful lizard foraged on the creek bed around my feet, occasionally even brushing against my knees. I snapped this shot and many like it on one of the several occasions where the animal surfaced for a breath and most likely to check that I wasn't acting suspiciously.

PHOTOGRAPHIC EQUIPMENT USED

Canon 5D III, 150-600mm Sigma, natural light.

SPECIES

Mitchell's Water Monitor (*Varanus mitchelli*)

PHOTOGRAPHER

Lachlan Gilding

STATUS

EX   EW   **CR**   EN   VU   NT   LC

LOCATION

Edith Falls, Northern Territory

NOTES

Total length 70cm. Like many predators in the top end, this species suffered serious impacts from the establishment of Cane Toads (*Rhinella marina*) in Australia. Current estimates suggest that this species underwent a decline of 80 per cent over an 18-year period. Thankfully, there is reasonable anecdotal evidence of the beginnings of a recovery, although until this is confirmed other threats need to be effectively managed.

STORY BEHIND THE PHOTO

Travelling through the Top End of the Northern Territory in summer can be arduous and tiring, so any chance to stop, relax and swim is always welcome. In my opinion one of the best spots to do that is Edith Falls. This is a stunning area that sports not only some incredible habitat but also some unique reptile species, including the endangered Mitchell's Water Monitor.

Despite once being a common sight along the pristine creek lines of northern Australia, the Mitchell's Water Monitor is unfortunately becoming increasingly uncommon due to the spread of the toxic Cane Toad.

I have visited Edith Falls on multiple occasions over the years and had never been lucky enough to see this species, likely due to its decline in the area. Despite all this I knew that the species still occurred here and I was determined to find one.

During March 2019 I was brought in to help film a documentary on reptiles with an Animal Planet production team, and one of the stops I had scheduled for this trip was the beautiful Edith Falls. After arriving in the area, we set out in search of the always common Mertens' Water Monitor, not expecting to find the less common Mitchell's Water Monitor instead, but nevertheless after climbing up a few waterfalls and walking up the creek line to a more untouched area we came across this individual. Of course, as I didn't expect to come across this species, I didn't have my camera and so I had to borrow one of the crew's in order to get this photo.

PHOTOGRAPHIC EQUIPMENT USED

Canon 5D IIII, Canon 100–400mm, natural light.

SPECIES

Rusty Monitor (*Varanus semiremex*)

PHOTOGRAPHER

Matt Summerville

STATUS

EX   EW   CR   EN   VU   NT   **LC**

LOCATION

Cairns, Queensland

NOTES

Total length 60cm. The widespread eradication of mangrove ecosystems throughout the species' range is the major threat, and it has been estimated that the range has contracted by almost 25 per cent. It seems that this species doesn't tolerate degraded habitat, and no animals are recorded under these conditions. Almost half of the range is under threat from residential development. The area has experienced an unprecedented housing boom in the past two decades and many species associated with mangroves are now under pressure.

STORY BEHIND THE PHOTO

This particular photo was taken on 8 December 2013, which is not at all a pleasant time of year to walk around mangroves in the tropics. There's a lot of sweat, sand flies and cut up feet. This was actually my first-ever Rusty Monitor in the wild, not long after moving to the Cairns area, and I was lucky enough to experience it with my favourite American – Hank the Yank, aka Zozizle, aka Stephen 'Heteronotia' Zozaya. I picked Stephen up from the airport and we decided to do a run to try and track down an elusive, crab-eating goanna. After circling Cairns, and the greater Cairns region, at least a dozen times we settled on a spot that looked good for a monitor lizard that thrives where most others would want to pack up and leave pretty quick. After trudging through the mangroves in the scorching sun for what seemed like an eternity, but only ended up being less than half an hour, we caught glimpse of our target making a poor effort to hide in what could only be described as a twig. Excitement quickly took over, we forgot about our bleeding shins, we high fived, hugged for no more than three seconds and then ran towards our prize. What a prize it was! So many shades of grey.

We proceeded to photograph what was a surprisingly cooperative lizard (especially compared to some of the ones I've come across since). After a quick photography session which was made to feel so much longer by the millions of insects eating us alive, we let the little goanna go on his way, and he was quick to run at high speed across the sand, jump into the water, swim in circles multiple times, exit the water, and then proceed to wedge himself inside a dead piece of timber with his legs and tail hanging out. The perfect hiding spot.

We were pretty happy with our find, and commenced the very short walk through the mud and mangroves back to the car – animals are always so close to the car after you've walked kilometres looking for them.

PHOTOGRAPHIC EQUIPMENT USED

Nikon D5000, Tamron 11–18mm wide-angle lens with broken autofocus and stuck on 11mm. Edited in Lightroom.

SPECIES

Lace Monitor (*Varanus varius*)

PHOTOGRAPHER

Shane Black

STATUS

EX EW CR EN VU NT **LC**

LOCATION

Wonga Beach, far north Queensland

NOTES

Total length 2.1m. Australia's second-largest lizard, and probably the one most recognised by many Australians. A common sight along the entire east coast of Australia, they have learnt that parks and picnic grounds can provide an easy meal, and can often be seen foraging for food scraps.

STORY BEHIND THE PHOTO

This photograph was taken on 26 September 2016. I had been living on acreage at Wonga Beach for a while when one day we found a juvenile Lace Monitor in our house. I was sitting in the lounge watching TV one day, when all of a sudden this little goanna just casually walked across the floor in front of me like he owned the place. I promptly caught him and released him outside thinking that would be the last time I saw him. I was wrong.

Over the next few months my girlfriend and I would see him regularly around the property, usually climbing the walls of the house, or casually walking past in the yard. Then one evening I noticed him climbing a large coconut tree in the yard. He climbed right to the top and then vanished into a hole amongst the fronds for the night. I had discovered where he was sleeping each night.

The next morning I ventured out to see if my little mate was around as I wanted to get a photo or two of him. He was nowhere to be seen. So I went off to do some work around the yard hoping he would pop up somewhere later in the day.

An hour or two later my dog started to carry on at the base of the coconut tree and I knew this little character had shown his face. I took the dog inside and grabbed my camera. I propped myself on the base of the tree and started taking some pics of him staring down at me.

What happened next I wasn't expecting… He slowly started to climb down the trunk towards me. I was expecting him to stop at a considerable distance from me, but he just kept coming. When he was just out of reach of me, he stopped. Then he fully stretched out, flattening his body in the process, and started basking in the morning sun. From where I was positioned I had a really unique perspective of this brave little lizard enjoying himself, showing off the beautiful black and yellow banding on his neck and stomach. He continued to bask for about 20 minutes until he had warmed up sufficiently to carry on with his daily business of finding insects and lizards to eat.

I really enjoy this image as it's such an unusual perspective, and it also reminds me of this bold little fella that came into my life. I still occasionally think of him, hoping he is doing well.

PHOTOGRAPHIC EQUIPMENT USED

Nikon D800, Sigma 150–400 lens, f5.6, 1/500s, ISO 125.

SPECIES

Woma (*Aspidites ramsayi*)

PHOTOGRAPHER

Steve Swanson

STATUS

EX EW CR EN VU NT **LC**

LOCATION

Port Hedland, Western Australia

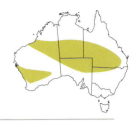

NOTES

Total length 1.1–3m, depending on locality. The largest are from South Australia, while specimens from Western Australia tend to be the smallest. The Woma and the closely related Black-headed Python (*A. melanocephalus*) are the only two species of python that lack heat-sensing pits.

STORY BEHIND THE PHOTO

It was a warm night in December 2010 and I was driving on a station track near Port Hedland in the company of a friend who is a licenced reptile collector. Geckos of various species were active on the track and it wasn't long before we encountered this beautiful Woma crossing our path.

Early the next morning I took the snake back into bushland to take some photos. I selected an area of typical Woma habitat, a sandy plain dominated by Poverty Bush. As Womas generally are, this specimen had a very placid disposition and presented no difficulty to photograph. Womas have a wide distribution across most of arid Australia and there is considerable variation between the populations. I consider the Pilbara Womas to be the most attractive of all.

PHOTOGRAPHIC EQUIPMENT USED

Pentax K10D, Sigma 18–50mm, f13, flash sync speed 1/180s, external flashgun mounted on camera hotshoe. Some minor adjustments to the image using Photoshop.

SPECIES

Centralian Carpet Python (*Morelia bredli*)

PHOTOGRAPHER

Max Jackson

STATUS

EX EW CR EN VU NT **LC**

LOCATION

Macdonnell Ranges, Northern Territory

NOTES

Total length 2.5m. One of the larger species within the carpet python complex, it's often the girth of these gentle giants that makes them so impressive. Found among rocky outcrops of inland Australia. Alternative name Bredl's Python. Described by well-known herpetologist Graeme Gow in 1981, the snake was named after his friend and fellow herpetologist Joe Bredl, who's son Rob – 'The Barefoot Bushman' – is carrying on the family tradition to this day.

STORY BEHIND THE PHOTO

This photo will always be a great memory for me as I will never forget the excitement when I first laid eyes upon this snake. The Centralian Carpet Python had been a species that had eluded me for many years despite me having passed through their distribution multiple times. This was my very last species of Australian python to see in the wild so I had high hopes when I put aside three nights in late October 2018 to scour the Macdonnell Ranges in search of one. The first two days and nights proved to be as unsuccessful as my previous attempts to see this species and I was definitely feeling the pressure as I set out for my final night in the centralian escarpments. A Desert Death Adder (*Acanthopis pyrrhus*), a sleeping Black-headed Monitor (*Varanus tristis*) and a large Mulga Snake (*Pseudechis australis*) kept my excitement up throughout the evening, however there was still no sign of *M. bredli*.

As I made my way back to the car I got an enormous thrill when I spotted a large 2m-long orange snake sitting in a large pond at the base of an escarpment. Not only had I found my target species, but in doing so I had managed to tick off the final member of the Pythonidae family in Australia. The Centralian Carpet Python was extremely accommodating and sat like an absolute gem as I got a couple of photos before heading back to the car after a very successful night.

PHOTOGRAPHIC EQUIPMENT USED

Canon 7D Mark II, Tokina 11–16mm, Twin Flash Canon EX 480, f13, 1/250s, ISO 100, 11mm. Edited in Lightroom.

SPECIES

Rough-scaled Python (*Morelia carinata*)

PHOTOGRAPHER

Lachlan Gilding

STATUS

EX   EW   CR   EN   VU   NT   **LC**

LOCATION

Kimberley Region, Western Australia

NOTES

Total length 2m. The only species of python in the world with keeled scales and forward-directed eyes. Remarkably similar to the Green Python, with which it shares a very close kinship as evidenced by molecular studies of the Australian pythons. These two species are the most arboreal of pythons, meaning that they prefer to spend most of their time off the ground in branches.

Until the end of the 20th century the Rough-scaled Python was known only from a few preserved specimens, until John Weigel from the Australian Reptile Park was able to locate and then breed a handful of wild-caught animals. In two decades the species has transformed from almost mythical status to now being one of the most commonly kept pythons in Australia.

STORY BEHIND THE PHOTO

Rough-scaled Pythons are without doubt one of the 'Holy Grail' species of the herpetological community. Since I was a kid I had stared at their photos in the field guide and dreamed of finding one in the wild. In 2016, I set off with a friend into the northern Kimberley in search of this species, and despite searching through the night for days on end we went away empty handed.

Despite this we started immediately planning our return for the following year, in October 2017. Once again we headed north into the remote Kimberley region of Western Australia. This time however, we chose a new location, Prince Regent National Park. After arriving in the late afternoon we were greeted with heavy rain which continued into the early hours of the night. Once the rain subsided we headed out in search of the Rough-scaled Python. After several hours of searching through the rocky boulder country I starting to give up hope of finding this elusive species. As I was trying to find my way back to the track I was using I heard a 'thump' behind me, I turned around to see a small python that had just fallen out of the tree above my head… It was a Rough-scaled Python.

PHOTOGRAPHIC EQUIPMENT USED

Canon 7D, Tokina 11–16mm wide angle, two external flashes, soft box.

SPECIES

Murray/Darling Carpet Python (*Morelia spilota metcalfei*)

PHOTOGRAPHER

Matt Summerville

STATUS

EX EW CR EN VU NT **LC**

LOCATION

Flinders Ranges, South Australia

NOTES

Total length 2.5m. Although the IUCN Red List has this species as Least Concern, it is listed as Endangered in Victoria, and its population in New South Wales is also under severe threat due to land clearance, grazing by domestic stock, a reduction in the number of hollow logs, and other forms of habitat degradation, as well as by poor management of the region's limited water supply.

STORY BEHIND THE PHOTO

On 29 January 2019 myself and a good mate, Mark 'one last lap' Green, decided that we'd do a bit of a detour on our drive from Kangaroo Island to Sydney and spend a night in the beautiful Flinders Ranges region of South Australia looking for Carpet Pythons. I'd only ever seen one Murray/Darling Carpet in the wild before, and it was a hatchling (and we all know they don't count) so I was determined to see a big adult!

At dusk the temperature plummeted quickly, and we did a quick lap of the road and got nothing but disappointment and the sight of one kangaroo eating another kangaroo, so we decided we would walk one of the unreal-looking gorges that are strewn throughout the Flinders in the hope that a snake may be out braving the cooler temperatures. I've also been told by many people that I have a warped sense of what's actually cold from years of living in northern Australia, but I'm fairly certain that I saw a snowflake fall from the sky that night.

Surprisingly though, not long after we walked into the gorge we were greeted by easily the nicest Carpet Python I have ever seen sprawled out among the rocks and fallen timber. Greeny let out what I can only describe as a high pitched 'yelp' as he scrambled to get out the words 'Murray/Darling!' We were beyond stoked to find this snake and quickly got to photographing it in the best way to show its incredible colouration, but in true Carpet Python fashion it wouldn't sit still for more than a quarter of a second, so being the extremely impatient photographer I am I decided that I'd let it curl up among the rocks on its own accord (anyone that knows anything about snakes knows just how simple a task that is...) and take a few photos looking down on the snake to try and show just how pretty this particular individual actually was. Once we finally both got a few photos we whispered a few kind words to the snake, packed up our camera gear and walked back to camp feeling pretty chuffed.

PHOTOGRAPHIC EQUIPMENT USED

Nikon D610 with a Nikon 60mm f/2.8 macro lens. Edited in Lightroom.

SPECIES

Diamond Python (*Morelia spilota spilota*)

PHOTOGRAPHER

Ken Griffiths

STATUS

EX   EW   CR   EN   VU   NT   **LC**

LOCATION

Captive individual, New South Wales

NOTES

Total length 3m. This southern relative of the carpet pythons, which are a common sight along many urban areas of the east coast, often turns up in and around houses. Although not under immediate threat, its range is also restricted to some of Australia's most increasingly developed areas, and they will continue to be under increasing pressure from habitat destruction. Rather drab looking as hatchlings, but after they have shed their skin a few times and get close to 1m in length they transform into one of the world's most beautiful snakes. Their good looks are equalled by their placid temperament and they are regarded as one of the most gentle species within the carpet python complex.

STORY BEHIND THE PHOTO

One of my favourite species of snake is the Diamond Python. I keep them in outdoor aviary enclosures and this suits them perfectly as they have total control over their thermal requirements. Most years one of my three females usually becomes gravid and they produce 20 or so eggs. I place them into an incubator where they usually take about 60 days, give or take a few, at a temperature of 28–30°C.

It is always a delight when they begin to hatch as it gives me plenty of opportunity to take photographs of the whole process. In this photograph I took a series of 23 photos which allows me to get a depth of field that will get both snakes in total focus. The process can be tedious and time consuming but when it works well the results are very rewarding.

PHOTOGRAPHIC EQUIPMENT USED

Canon 6D Mark II, 100mm f2.8L macro lens, atural diffused light, f6.3, 1/200s, ISO 640. Minor adjustments and sharpening in Adobe Photoshop CS6.

SPECIES

Green Python (*Morelia viridis*)

PHOTOGRAPHER

Chris Jolly

STATUS

EX EW CR EN VU NT **LC**

LOCATION

Kutini-Payamu (Iron Range) National Park, Queensland

NOTES

Total length 1.8m. One of the most iconic reptiles of the Australian wet tropics. Also found in New Guinea, with some taxonomists suggesting that there are likely multiple species yet to be described. This species has an impressive colour change (referred to as an ontogenetic change), where hatchling snakes emerge as one colour before transitioning to striking green as adults. Australian specimens are all yellow as hatchlings, however internationally several colour varieties exist, including red neonates.

STORY BEHIND THE PHOTO

This photo was taken in October 2016, during a herping and birding trip with Max Jackson and Lockie Gilding. I had been to this incredible rainforest national park on the Cape York Peninsula the previous year and found this species within minutes while walking around near camp on the first night. Having driven the 13 hours from Cairns to get there earlier that morning, and feeling less than enthusiastic to set my camera up, I opted to wait until the following night to photograph the species. As is often the case when you're lazy as a photographer and don't take the shot when it is presented to you, I hiked around for the following three nights without seeing another Green Python. I left elated that I had finally seen the species, but disappointed I had been too lazy on the first night to photograph it.

So when the opportunity to head back to Kutini-Payamu (Iron Range) National Park the following year, despite having just started a PhD and having neither the time nor the money for such a trip, I had no choice but to take it. As was the case on the previous trip, we found the species fairly rapidly on the first night. I wasn't going to miss this opportunity.

PHOTOGRAPHIC EQUIPMENT USED

Canon 7D, Canon 60mm macro, Canon 430EX II twin speedlites and Adobe Lightroom.

SPECIES

Amethystine Python (*Simalia kinghorni*)

PHOTOGRAPHER

Jiri Herout

STATUS

EX EW CR EN VU NT **LC**

LOCATION

Cairns, Queensland

NOTES

Total length 4m, although one individual of 8.5m was recorded. More commonly referred to as Scrub Python. Within Australia restricted to northern tropical Queensland, although also found in parts of Indonesia, New Guinea and surrounding islands. In Australia they prefer dense warm rainforests, spending much of their time high in trees — a somewhat unusual trait for a species so large. They are also frequent visitors to homes in the Cairns region and will often make a meal of pet birds and the occasional cat. They have also been known to eat small kangaroos and wallabies.

STORY BEHIND THE PHOTO

I visit Cairns every year as it is common knowledge that this part of Queensland has far more reptiles and amphibians compared to my home area of Sydney and its surroundings in New South Wales. During one of these visits, following a hot and sticky day on 21 April 2017, I decided to go night herping with my mates. The feeling of the torch on my head, the fresh air and the silence of nature around me is what I love the most and it calms me deeply.

We were herping all night long and on the way back, just a five-minute walk from the house that we rented, we came across this beautiful Amethystine Python lying on the ground. Also known as the Scrub Python, this species is one of the longest non-venomous reptiles in Australia with an average length of 3.5–4m for a full-grown adult. The longest one ever found was reputedly more than 8m long.

Most pythons are nocturnal but these snakes may sometimes be observed sunning themselves during the day. The rainforest is so dense that the sun's rays rarely penetrate through to the ground, so most pythons tend to bask in the treetops. This species is very slender compared to most other pythons, to enable it to move through the trees easily. It is found mainly in the eastern part of the Cape York Peninsula, feeding on mammals and birds. It is very rare python and I feel very lucky to have had the opportunity to observe and photograph it.

PHOTOGRAPHIC EQUIPMENT USED

Canon EOS 5D Mark 3, Canon 17–40mm f/4L USM, Canon 580 Mark 2 flash, f10, 1/200s, ISO 100. This photo was tricky to capture, but the key to success was diffusers – I used two external diffusers, one on the lens and the second on top of the flash so it dispersed the light. I selected a focal length of 40mm because with this wide-angle lens 17mm would have been too rounded. The process was a little bit challenging, but with a very satisfactory result.

SPECIES

Arafura File Snake (*Acrochordus arafurae*)

PHOTOGRAPHER

Etienne Littlefair

STATUS

EX EW CR EN VU NT **LC**

LOCATION

Katherine area, Northern Territory

NOTES

Total length up to 2.5m. Members of the file snake family are all highly specialised aquatic species. They get their name from the unusual rough file-like skin. This helps them to grip slippery fish, which make up the bulk of their diet. The loose-fitting skin also means that they can eat fish much larger than their own girth, however this makes moving on land an awkward and slow process. Females are usually larger than males and give birth to up to 27 young every two or three years.

STORY BEHIND THE PHOTO

This photo was taken on 4 June 2018 around 10.30am. Arafura File Snakes are common inhabitants of waterways across the Top End, Gulf, and northern Queensland, where they feed predominantly on small to medium-sized fish and are in turn prey for crocodiles, waterbirds, larger fish and Australian Aboriginal peoples, for whom in some areas these snakes are an important source of protein. In the dry season these snakes can be found in huge abundance in certain permanent bodies of water, where they await the monsoonal rains that allow them to disperse onto seasonal floodplains and fatten up for the following dry.

As well as being a hugely important part of ecosystems and Aboriginal culture, these snakes are also the largest and most common of Australia's freshwater aquatic snakes that I encounter in the water. The Little File Snake (*Acrochordus granulatus*) more typically inhabits brackish waters and mangroves, firmly in the domain of Saltwater Crocodiles; while I only infrequently encounter the smaller and more secretive Macleay's Water Snake (*Pseudoferania polylepis*). When I set out to photograph Arafura File Snakes I planned a photo that revealed the snake's typical habitat and yet focused closely on its head and seemingly perpetually visible tongue.

Such a photo would show all the key features of the snake, particularly the granular file-like skin, for which they were named.

A subsequent challenge was the often nocturnal behaviour of these snakes – they can be difficult to locate during the day when they remain hidden away in deep root systems and burrows along creek banks. To overcome this I sought to take this image in the dry season when cooler water temperatures tempt snakes into the open during the day to enjoy the sun's warmth. A photographic challenge with this type of image is depth of field – reptile photographers always want more for in-habitat style photos. To achieve appropriate depth for this image I used a fisheye lens, something I am loath to do above water. However, as the saying goes, it's a whole other world underwater, there are few straight lines and so fisheye distortions are permissible to my tastes and add to the underwater enchantment. This image is not quite what I had in mind when I set out, yet it reveals the root systems in which these snakes are often found, the blue skies of the dry season and the fascinatingly unique features of the snake. I will certainly be back in the water once the water temperatures begin to cool.

PHOTOGRAPHIC EQUIPMENT USED

Olympus EM1 Mark II with Olympus 8mm f1.8 lens, Nauticam housing, Sea and Sea strobes. Processed using Adobe Photoshop CC.

SPECIES

Brown Tree Snake (*Boiga irregularis*)

PHOTOGRAPHER

Scott Eipper

STATUS

EX   EW   CR   EN   VU   NT   **LC**

LOCATION

Brisbane, Queensland

NOTES

Total length 2m. As the name suggests, this species is a skilled climber and spends most of its time either in rock escarpments or in trees. A rear-fanged species which is venomous but not considered a threat to humans. It is nocturnal and feeds mainly on birds, bats and other small mammals.

Introduced to the Pacific island of Guam just after World War II as stowaways in US military equipment. The population exploded and it is estimated that there are now 2 million individuals on the island, with each square kilometre holding up to 5,000. The consequences of the introduction were that 10 of the 12 native bird species in Guam disappeared by the mid-1980s, and fruit bat populations diminished greatly as well. Because two-thirds of tree species on the island require animals to disperse and germinate their seeds, this devastating reduction in flying animals has reduced new forest growth by 61–92 per cent.

STORY BEHIND THE PHOTO

Brisbane's subtropical climate, coupled with green belts and waterways, allows wildlife to penetrate even the inner-city regions. After hearing about a good population of a couple species of native geckos, I set off hoping to get a shot of a Robust Velvet Gecko (*Nebulifera robusta*) with the Brisbane skyline in the background. I drove to the various lookouts around Brisbane hoping to see a native gecko when I came across a stunning Brown Tree Snake sitting at the end of a branch. To say I was happy was an understatement after seeing only Asian House Geckos (*Hemidactylus frenatus*) and Cane Toads (*Rhinella marina*).

My camera was already mounted onto a tripod and I had the settings already figured out from taking some test shots earlier in the night. I did not want to guess when I had an animal sitting in front of me as I knew it was going to be a case of only getting maybe one or two chances to get the shot.

I set the camera in front of the snake, which sat immobile while I focused the lens. I placed the camera into timer mode and pressed the shutter. I pressed the test button on the diffused flash twice about a second apart from opposing sides of the snake. This exposed the foreground while the length of the time exposed the remaining background in the image. The image was then post-processed to correct levels and other minor aspects.

PHOTOGRAPHIC EQUIPMENT USED

Nikon D300, Nikkor 18–77 mm telephoto, one Nikon SB800 flash diffused with tissue paper – pulsed twice in test mode during exposure, f8, 1/3s, ISO 100, +1 step.

SPECIES

Common Tree Snake (*Dendrelaphis punctulatus*)

PHOTOGRAPHER

Lachlan Gilding

STATUS

EX   EW   CR   EN   VU   NT   **LC**

LOCATION

Kimberley Region, Western Australia

NOTES

Total length up to 2m. This species is highly variable in colour and can be olive-green, or golden like this individual, while some populations are a stunning sky blue. They have no fangs, no venom and are very reluctant to bite. Active during the day, foraging primarily for frogs, lizards, small mammals and even fish. They have large eyes and keen eyesight. During winter it's quite common for groups of these snakes congregate together in order to conserve heat.

STORY BEHIND THE PHOTO

The Common Tree Snake is one of the most variable species Australia has to offer, with individuals existing in almost every colour you can imagine. Coming from south-east Queensland I was very used to finding this species in its typical forms – black or grey with a pale yellow belly – and until this point I had never come across the golden variation of tree snake from northern Australia.

In late 2016 I was travelling with a few friends from the east coast across on to the Kimberley region of Western Australia on our annual crocodile research trip. Unfortunately, whilst driving along the Barkley Highway, our air-conditioning failed and so we were stuck crossing the country in summer with no AC. To combat the discomfort we were stopping at every water hole we could find. Eventually we came across a beautifully clear water hole beside the Victoria Highway. Whilst cooling off in the clear blue water we heard something drop out of one of the *Pandanus* trees behind us, and we quickly turned around to find this stunning golden tree snake sitting on the surface of the water staring back at us. After taking a few quick photos, the animal cruised back to its safe home in the *Pandanus*.

PHOTOGRAPHIC EQUIPMENT USED

Canon 7D, Tokina 11–16mm wide angle, two external flashes.

SPECIES

Oriental Wolf Snake (*Lycodon capucinus*)

PHOTOGRAPHER

Hal Cogger

STATUS

EX EW CR EN VU NT **LC**

LOCATION

The Pink House, Christmas Island, Indian Ocean

NOTES

Total length 70cm. Harmless to humans. Feeds primarily on lizards. Has a huge range throughout South-East Asia and the Pacific. Not native to Australia or New Zealand, but introduced to Christmas Island – another tragic example of the damage an interloper can do to an unprepared ecosystem.

STORY BEHIND THE PHOTO

In 1988 Laurie Smith at the Western Australian Museum reported the recent arrival on Christmas Island of the Oriental Wolf Snake, *Lycodon capucinus*, a well-known predator on small lizards. At first it appeared to be largely confined to the town area in the north-eastern part of the island, and it was hoped that it would concentrate its numbers in this area where it would benefit from the abundance of recently introduced geckos – the House Gecko (*Hemidactylus frenatus*) and the Skin-shedding Dtella (*Gehyra mutilata*), as well as the rats and mice that were in abundance in the town.

In 1979 Ross Sadlier and I had found the endemic Christmas Island Blue-tailed Skink (*Cryptoblepharus egeriae*) to be extremely common in the town area. By the time of our next island survey in 1998, the Blue-tailed skinks had disappeared. The wolf snake was tentatively blamed for this decline, and for the apparent decline of several other Christmas Island native lizards. The evidence was sparse, but some other native lizards still seemed to be thriving. For example, in 1998, on the trunk of a single large rainforest tree that had apparently been brought down by a storm, Ross and I counted more than 80 large endemic Forest Skinks (*Emoia nativitatis*) before we gave up counting as newcomers milled about with those already counted. Yet the last of Christmas Island's Forest Skinks died in captivity only 16 years later, in May 2014.

Now, about 30 years after the wolf snake was first introduced to Christmas Island, only one of island's native lizards survives in the wild – the Christmas Island Forest Gecko (*Cyrtodactylus sadlerii*). The wolf snake, together with an introduced giant centipede (*Scolopendra subspinipes*) and the invasive introduced Yellow Crazy Ant (*Anoplolepis gracilipes*), are widely regarded as collectively responsible for the loss of the native lizards, although the wolf snake is usually assigned major responsibility – on logical rather than evidentiary grounds. The snake itself is a colourful, nocturnal, oviparous colubrid with great climbing ability. I have seen them high on the trunks of large rainforest trees.

Attempts elsewhere in the world to control and/or eliminate snakes from such complex habitats have rarely proved effective and island faunas everywhere have been highly susceptible to the impacts of the accidental introduction of new predators. Christmas Island, with a rich endemic fauna due to its long isolation, has been highly impacted by human-assisted exotic species. The consequence for Australian herpetology has been that Christmas Island has the honour of recording the first three extinctions, in the wild, of any Australian reptile species. Two have a chance of survival if captive animals can be successfully reintroduced to the island. But one – the Forest Skink – has apparently gone forever. All due in large part to the impacts of this invasive little snake. It is to be hoped that it never reaches the Australian mainland.

PHOTOGRAPHIC EQUIPMENT USED

Nikon D5000 camera using a 60mm Micro Nikor lens and the camera's built-in flash, ISO 100.

SPECIES

Macleay's Water Snake (*Pseudoferania popylepis*)

PHOTOGRAPHER

Michael Cermak

STATUS

EX EW CR EN VU NT **LC**

LOCATION

Cairns, north Queensland

NOTES

A stocky little snake, maximum total length 80cm. Rear-fanged and weakly venomous. Rarely bites and not considered dangerous to humans. Live-bearing, giving birth to around 11 offspring. Quite awkward on land but graceful in water. Found in freshwater billabongs, streams and mangrove swamps across the top end of Australia. Opportunistic predator of most smaller animals that occupy the waterways, including fish, eels and frogs. Sole species in the genus *Pseudoferania*, which was reinstated in 2011 as genetic testing suggested that the species is only distantly related to the genus *Enhydris* from South-East Asia.

STORY BEHIND THE PHOTO

A couple of years ago the kids from two doors down brought me a present. They knew I was into reptiles so they brought me this 'water snake' they caught in Freshwater Creek on the outskirts of Cairns. I was keeping aquarium fish at the time and I had a spare tank set up on the back porch with a few rainbow fish in it. I put the snake in and went to get my camera and lights. When I got back the water was murky as the snake enthusiastically explored this new environment, so I decided to let everything settle down and do the shoot the next day.

In the morning the water was clear as crystal but there was no sign of my rainbows – I knew straightaway what had happened. Having all my gear set up, I sat down and waited for the snake to come up for a breath of air when I noticed that the glass wasn't really clean, either inside and out, so another delay was inevitable because I stirred up the sediments while wiping algae off the glass. Some hours later everything finally looked good and to my pleasant surprise the snake was slowly cruising around, not reacting to my presence near the tank, nor it reacted to my firing three flashguns into its face. When taking photographs through glass, it's important to point the lens directly against the glass to avoid distortion and the rainbow effect. It's also important to make sure there is no reflection of the lens (sometimes even the photographer) in the front glass. All set, and after a few test shots to get the lighting right I was ready shoot. When the session was over, I placed the snake into a wet bag and drove to the spot where the kids caught it and released it there. I also took a scoop net with me in case I see some rainbows to replace the ones the snake had eaten.

PHOTOGRAPHIC EQUIPMENT USED

Canon 1Ds Mark III, Canon 24–70mm L 2.8 lens, three Canon Speedlite EX600EX-RT flashguns, f16, 1/60s, ISO 100.

SPECIES

Common Death Adder (*Acanthophis antarcticus*)

PHOTOGRAPHER

Jason Luke

STATUS

EX   EW   CR   EN   VU   NT   **LC**

LOCATION

Heathcote, New South Wales

NOTES

Total length 1m, although a 1.2m specimen was recorded in 2019. Dangerously venomous. Australia's ultimate ambush predator. There are several species of death adder found in Australia and all have evolved an ingenious method of catching a meal. Generally stout, heavy-bodied species, they all have a small, slender tail that looks remarkably like a worm or caterpillar. Buried under leaves or sand to avoid detection, the snake strategically places its tail just in front of its head, wriggling it in the hope of attracting a bird or small lizard. When the inquisitive prospective meal arrives the snake strikes with surprising speed and holds its prey until the venom immobilises it moments later.

STORY BEHIND THE PHOTO

The Common Death Adder is always a welcome find by those who love and photograph reptiles. Within the Sydney Basin they come in two main colour morphs: grey and red. Whilst being dangerously venomous they are pretty easy to work with for those with experience in dealing with venomous snakes. The majority of the ones I've found have been very relaxed snakes despite their fearsome-sounding name. I don't find that many of them locally around my home turf in southern Sydney, maybe one or two a year. They are far more prevalent to the north and on the western edges of Sydney.

I found this particular red-morph individual whilst doing a night walk along one of my local trails in Heathcote National Park on 3 March 2018. The weather had been quite warm and I thought a night walk might turn up something of interest. I didn't have to wait very long. I was only about 1.5km into my usual 14km walk when I saw the death adder on the edge of the track, moving through some small shrubs at approximately 6.30pm. I couldn't believe my luck and quickly found a stick and herded the snake to a clearing a couple of metres away. I was being careful not to aggravate it as that would make photography more difficult. I managed to settle it down next to a log at the edge of a clearing which would make a good backdrop for the photo. This particular snake was very well behaved and photographed easily. It's always a joy to work with such snakes. Although the start of the night was promising, I didn't find anything else during my walk. I wasn't worried though – I was extremely happy to have had the opportunity to photograph this magnificent snake. I used an on-camera speed light (1/1) with a soft box and second lens-mounted screen diffuser and a second mini tripod-mounted remote speed light (1/2) with soft box set to light the background. I prefer my night shots to have a dark mood about them and I feel this shot captures that mood perfectly.

PHOTOGRAPHIC EQUIPMENT USED

Nikon D800, Sigma 24mm ART f/1.4, two Nikon SB910 Speedlights with Lastolight soft boxes and Interfit Strobies Diffuser, Promaster mini tripod, f16, 1/250s, ISO 100, 24mm. Image adjusted on iPhoto.

SPECIES

Highland Copperhead (*Austrelaps ramsayi*)

PHOTOGRAPHER

Peter Soltys

STATUS

EX   EW   CR   EN   VU   NT   **LC**

LOCATION

Wollongong, New South Wales

NOTES

Total length 1.3m. One of the only species that has benefited from European settlement as areas converted from forest to farmland introduced wetter environments in which this species to thrives. As the name suggests, it lives in highland areas of New South Wales and eastern Victoria, and it is one of the few species of snake that can withstand the cold, moist environments in these places. Feeds mainly on ectothermic prey such as frogs, lizards and insects, with skinks being favoured. Reported to be cannibalistic.

STORY BEHIND THE PHOTO

This photo was taken on 10 February 2018 near the city of Wollongong. It was just another ordinary herping day. My colleague and I were scouting the location for a White-lipped Snake early in the morning. As we were walking out of the car park we came across this wonderful stretch of road where the sun was cutting through the trees and creating beautiful sun patches on the ground.

I thought to myself that this would make a cool spot for a photo, and said to my colleague, "How cool it would be to find….", and before I managed to finish the sentence, he said "SNAKE!". At that moment the morning quickly escalated from being ordinary to epic.

After a quick discussion where I explained what shot I had in mind, we found the perfect spot. The trick was to use those sun patches on the background for the contrast. However, there was still too much sun hitting the snake and that would create burn spots on the scales. In contrast to my colleague, I am a person who does not enjoy spending time editing photos. Quick colour correction is okay, however everything that takes more than five minutes kills me. I'd rather spend more time herping. I was also hoping to use a Canon Speedlight 600EX to bring up more details as well so I had to figure out how to take the shot without any direct sunlight. By putting diffusion next to the snake, I created a stronger shadow on it. I was slowly increasing the ISO to the point that the background was perfectly exposed and the snake was still in the shadow. And then I used my Canon Speedlight 600EX as a fill light in combination with two diffusions. All in all it was bit of a handful, but it was quick and so worth it. The photo you are looking at now is almost the same as it came out of the camera.

PHOTOGRAPHIC EQUIPMENT USED

Canon EOS 5D Mark IV, Canon EF 24mm L Mark II f 1.4, Canon Speedlight 600EX, combination of softbox and second diffusion, f18, 1/200s, ISO 640, flash setting: ETTL. Editing using Lightroom Classic.

SPECIES

Coppertail Whipsnake (*Demansia reticulata cupreiceps*)

PHOTOGRAPHER

Ross McGibbon

STATUS

EX EW CR EN VU NT **LC**

LOCATION

Laverton, Western Australia

NOTES

Total length 80cm. Bites from this venomous elapid are not considered life threatening. Not usually an aggressive species and tends to avoid contact with humans.

STORY BEHIND THE PHOTO

In October 2017, myself and fellow reptile enthusiast Tim Squires set off on an expedition into the remote Great Victoria Desert, about a 1,500km drive inland of Perth, Western Australia. On the way, we would pass through the Goldfields region of Western Australia. With high summer temperatures, an average annual rainfall of only 250mm and extremely arid soils, conditions are tough for the flora and fauna that manage to eke out an existence here. When it comes to reptiles in the Goldfields it's more about quality than quantity, and the most elegant snake in this region is the Coppertail Whipsnake. With its exceptional burnt-yellow and steel-blue markings, it was the snake I hoped to locate and photograph most while in the region.

Around 1,000km of driving brought us to a patch of habitat near Laverton where the hard stony soils merge with red sand and spinifex. This was the perfect habitat to search for this snake as the spinifex harbours an abundance of lizards for whipsnakes to prey on.

Like the majority of Australia's venomous snakes, whipsnakes are active foragers, so road cruising through their habitat was the most effective way to locate one. It's a huge game of luck, requiring us to be in exactly the right time and place to see one crossing or basking on the road. We commenced our search around 8am and over the course of a few hours we located a Thorny Devil (*Moloch horridus*) and a few Sand Monitors (*Varanus gouldii*). The day warmed up quickly and by midday it was 36°C and generally too hot for snakes to be active. During the heat of the day we focused our efforts on other more heat-tolerant reptiles such as the Goldfields Pebble-mimic Dragon (*Tympanocryptis pseudopsephos*) until the heat began to ease off around 4pm.

As we lapped the road again and again in search of a whipsnake I began to think that we weren't going to locate one before the sun went down. Our luck changed when just around the next bend I saw a long, thin shape on the road ahead. Before I could bring the car to a complete stop I could already tell what it was by its beautiful blue and yellow markings. It was exactly what we were looking for – a healthy Coppertail Whipsnake around 80cm long.

With daylight running out we repositioned the snake off the road to photograph it. I utilised my wide-angle lens to capture it in its natural habitat among the red sand and spinifex. I also orientated my frame to capture the setting sun in the background in order to depict the time of day the photograph was taken. The sun added another natural element to the image, as well as introducing some more colour into the horizon. After the sun and the whipsnake had disappeared, I reviewed my images and noticed that the colours in the afternoon sky almost completely matched those on the whipsnake.

PHOTOGRAPHIC EQUIPMENT USED

Canon 5D Mark III, Tamron 15–30mm wide-angle lens, external speedlight flash and diffuser. Post processing using Adobe Lightroom.

SPECIES

Shine's Whipsnake (*Demansia shinei*)

PHOTOGRAPHER

Max Jackson

STATUS

EX EW CR EN VU NT **LC**

LOCATION

Barkly region, Northern Territory

NOTES

Total Length 60cm. Named after Professor Richard Shine and also known as the Shiny Ricksnake. This small elapid inhabits arid and semiarid regions, where it is thought to feed primarily on small lizards.

STORY BEHIND THE PHOTO

In my opinion *Demansia* is one of Australia's more underrated genera of snakes. With 14 species spread across the continent it is extremely challenging for the herper to 'tick off' every species and the Shine's Whipsnake (*Demansia shinei*) is definitely one of the harder species to glimpse in the wild.

Over a period of five years I have made a number of trips into its red-sand/spinifex habitat in Australia's centre, however a single roadkill was the only specimen I was able to discover. Fortunately for me I was offered a fauna survey contract right in the centre of the species' distribution in May 2018, which I eagerly accepted in the hope that I'd finally come across this elusive species.

After a week's worth of walking 20km a day in the fly-infested country I was finally rewarded with this beautiful individual moving through the red sand on a cool winter morning. It was an absolute treat to photograph and I had trouble wiping the smile off my face as I saw it slither back into the spinifex.

PHOTOGRAPHIC EQUIPMENT USED

Canon 7D Mark II, Tamron 90mm, Twin Flash Canon EX 480, f14, 1/250s, ISO 100. Edited using Lightroom.

SPECIES

Collared Whipsnake (*Demansia torquata*)

PHOTOGRAPHER

Chris Jolly

STATUS

EX EW CR EN VU NT **LC**

LOCATION

Talaroo Station, Queensland

NOTES

Total length 50cm. Found in the tropical forest edges of Queensland. Fast moving and feeds primarily on lizards by actively chasing them down. Clutch size usually two to eight eggs. The name 'torquata' means collared.

STORY BEHIND THE PHOTO

This photo was taken in April 2016 during a biodiversity survey of Talaroo Station – a former cattle station that had recently been returned to the Ewamian traditional owners. Brendan Schembri and I were tasked with taking an inventory of the biodiversity of the property and had set up pit, funnel, Elliott and cage traps at sites in the various different habitats across the property. One morning, as we were driving out to check these traps, we noticed a small, slender snake rapidly crossing the dirt road. I slammed on the brakes and Brendan expertly dived from the car and caught the whipsnake before it disappeared into the grass.

The Aboriginal rangers we were working with were less than impressed when I told them we were bringing the snake with us to get tissue samples and photos. Unfortunately, in our haste to capture the snake and our excitement about finding a new species for the property, we forgot to record a GPS location of where we had collected the snake. In the front, we discussed with some shame what we were going to do because we had forgotten where on the 50km stretch of track we had found the snake and you always must return them to the exact site of capture. This was when an Aboriginal ranger in the back seat piped up and said: "I know where you got the bastard! Back that a' way, near that big ol' ironbark." We were on an expansive property entirely dominated by ironbarks, so I wasn't feeling hopeful that the snake would be returned to the site of capture… But sure enough, as we were driving back to camp the ranger sang out as we drove along a seemingly nondescript section of road: "This is where you got the bastard!" And from the back seat he proceeded to point out what we were clearly blind to. "See them skid marks where you locked up the brakes and scared the life outta us? And see, there's Brendan's tracks chasing that bloody snake into the grass. And there's our tracks running down the road." After a few quick photos the snake was returned to *exactly* where it had come from.

PHOTOGRAPHIC EQUIPMENT USED

Canon 7D, Canon 60mm macro, Canon 430EX II twin speedlites and Adobe Lightroom.

SPECIES

White-lipped Snake (*Drysdalia coronoides*)

PHOTOGRAPHER

Rob Valentic

STATUS

EX   EW   CR   EN   VU   NT   **LC**

LOCATION

Inverloch, South Gippsland, Victoria

NOTES

Total length 40cm. Usually considered harmless due to mild venom. Tolerant of cold. One of the few snake species found in Tasmania.

STORY BEHIND THE PHOTO

I love spending the early days of spring alone in the vast coastal swamps and salt marshes in the South Gippsland region of Victoria. The area offers a low diversity of species in contrast to much of mainland Australia, but the herping is special and unique. The only three snake species that occur here can be found with some consistency on mild or even cold days, so long as the winds are not too fierce. These are the White-lipped Snake, Lowland Copperhead (*Austrelaps superbus*) and Tiger Snake (*Notechis scutatus*).

Unlike in northern Australia, where many snakes are active at night, this style of herping is done on foot and during daylight, so it is entirely visual and therefore a little more immersive. It presents opportunities for a little indulgence, where one can move casually from one subject to the next without that sense of urgency associated with missing out on a species that is new and/or hard to find. I have a preference for overcast days with intermittent sunshine, as I can incorporate interesting cloud formations into the landscape and avoid highlight blowouts which are a problem on clear days with bright sun.

It was on one such day in early September 2018 that I travelled to an ephemeral coastal swamp near Inverloch. As all these snakes are very shy, wearing subdued clothing and treading lightly helps, as does ensuring that any shadow does not cause disturbance.

Slightly elevated mats of sedge and dieback vegetation afford the snakes a platform on which to bask. They exploit slight depressions on their surface and seek the protection of overhead tussocks both for wind breaks and to avoid detection from raptors flying overhead. They frequently bask partly concealed, and an exposed coil is often all one can see. As I moved slowly along a north-facing slope I had several partial views of copperheads that were dulled off for imminent shedding. I was stoked to see the snakes already basking at 9am in 12°C.

Moments later I spotted this large, clean and recently-shed female White-lipped Snake basking on the edge of a Wallaby Grass tussock. I was elated, as she was not a red morph in magnificent condition. Red is the least common of the three colour morphs here, with grey the most prevalent followed by olive-green. I gently plucked her up and moved her to a location in which I could best incorporate the entire habitat and the snake with a wide-angle lens.

I quickly settled on a bluff above a creek. I used the lowest flash output available on the Speedlite because the overcast conditions afford a very even subject illumination and I did not want to compromise the natural feel of the scene. I gentle placed the snake on the edge of the bluff on an overgrazed tussock and she was most obliging, allowing me to fine tune her into an appealing pose. I took a series of images and checked these on the viewer. I was so happy with the result and quickly abandoned the gear while I ran her back to where I found her.

PHOTOGRAPHIC EQUIPMENT USED

Canon 5D Mark IV DSLR, EF mount Venus Laowa 15/4 wide angle 1:1 lens, diffused external Canon Speedlite hotshoe mounted. Adobe Elements with Raw Plugin software.

SPECIES

Pale-headed Snake (*Hoplocephalus bitorquatus*)

PHOTOGRAPHER

Jules Farquhar

STATUS

EX   EW   CR   EN   VU   NT   **LC**

LOCATION

Lake Broadwater, Queensland

NOTES

Total length 60cm. Dangerously venomous. This species and the closely related Stephens' Banded Snake (*H. stephensii*) are Australia's only truly arboreal snakes which are considered dangerous to humans. Spend much of their time under bark, feeding mainly on geckos which share the same habitat.

STORY BEHIND THE PHOTO

On 3 February 2016 I flew to Sydney to meet up with some mates and embark on a ten-day herp crusade across north-east New South Wales and south-east Queensland. I was particularly excited because at the time I had never herped Queensland before, and our glovebox list of species to encounter was a tantalising reminder of how our efforts would be rewarded. On the third night of the trip we arrived at Lake Broadwater in south-east Queensland, which is home to a small arboreal elapid known as the Pale-headed Snake – one of the species I was most eager to see on the trip. Not long after searching the woodlands surrounding the lake, it began raining and my head-torch died, and so did my hopes of finding the snake. But when a Crucifix Frog (*Notaden bennetti*) appeared out of the mud in front of me I knew a fun night with the amphibians would suffice. We camped by the lake for the night and continued heading north early the next morning, feeling somewhat defeated but hopeful that we could still find a Pale-headed Snake elsewhere in the Brigalow Belt.

By 11 February it was the penultimate day of the trip and we had spent the past five days successfully herping the Brigalow Belt, but still with no Pale-headed Snake. We were just leaving the township of Dingo in the morning when one of us conceived the wild idea that if we made the seven-hour pilgrimage straight down to Lake Broadwater we could make it there by dusk and have a second chance of finding a Pale-headed Snake. So we found ourselves at Lake Broadwater again. This time there was no rain, it was warm and dry, and my head-torch was fully charged. Within an hour of searching the tree trunks and ground we found several Robust Velvet Geckos (*Nebulifera robusta*) and by 8pm we found a Pale-headed Snake on the ground beside a large tree. I got my camera out, set up the flashes and started taking pictures of the snake on a log. This species is known for its pugnacious attitude, so it wasn't long before it opened its mouth in an aposematic manner. I held one flash out in front of the snake with my left hand, while an offsider held another flash from above. I took a photo as it held its mouth open, and I was pleased with the resulting image. As we made our triumphant walk back to the car we found an active Dwyer's Snake (*Parasuta dwyeri*) on the ground in front of us. There was no time to photograph it, though – the night was young and there were more reptiles waiting for us three hours south at the granite hills of Girraween.

PHOTOGRAPHIC EQUIPMENT USED

Canon EOS 70D, Canon EF-S 60mm f/2.8 USM macro lens, f/18, 1/250s, ISO 100, RAW. The camera's built-in flash was used to trigger two hand-held Canon Speedlite flashes with diffusion softboxes. Minor adjustments to exposure were made using Adobe Lightroom.

SPECIES

Broad-headed Snake (*Hoplocephalus bungaroides*)

PHOTOGRAPHER

Chris Jolly

STATUS

EX   EW   CR   EN   **VU**   NT   LC

LOCATION

Blue Mountains, New South Wales

NOTES

Average total length 55cm, but specimens over 90cm have been recorded. Name originates from defence display – when threatened, the snake will flatten its head, making it wider. Distributed throughout the Sydney Basin of New South Wales, within a radius of about 250km from the city. Once quite common, but now listed as vulnerable due to increased urbanisation causing populations to decline. Feeds largely on lizards and frogs. Live-bearers, giving birth to 8–20 young per clutch.

STORY BEHIND THE PHOTO

This photo was taken in July 2013 and was the first wide-angle photo I ever attempted. The Broad-headed Snake is listed as endangered in New South Wales because it is a habitat specialist during the winter months, when it relies entirely on exfoliating caprock on the unvegetated edges of sandstone escarpments.

Unfortunately for this snake, its entire range centres on Australia's oldest and largest city, Sydney, and extends no more than 250km in any direction from the city. This has left it at the mercy of rampant urbanisation, bush rock collection and poaching.

This photo was taken during a study investigating the ecology of the species. Unfortunately, the Broad-headed Snake seems to be very sensitive to disturbance and has been lost from a lot of sites where it was formerly common, sometimes because of herp photographers unscrupulously turning the fragile caprock which the snakes rely upon for winter survival.

Since my passion for field herpetology started as a child, I have seen this species disappear from places where it could formerly be found, presumably because myself and other passionate herpers wanted to add it to their tick list. I have since become more aware of the unintended impact we can have following our passion, and because of this I now believe it is unethical to search for this species in winter, since this process requires the movement of tightly embedded caprock.

PHOTOGRAPHIC EQUIPMENT USED

Canon 60D, Canon 10–22mm wide angle, twin Canon 430EX II speedlites. Adobe Lightroom.

SPECIES

Western Tiger Snake (*Notechis scutatus occidentalis*)

PHOTOGRAPHER

Rob Valentic

STATUS

 EX   EW   CR   EN   VU   NT   **LC**

LOCATION

Gin Gin, Western Australia

NOTES

Total Length 1.2m. Often found around creeks, lagoons and other wetlands. Broad diet includes mammals, frogs, snakes, lizards and even carrion. Venom highly neurotoxic. Aggressive and dangerous to humans.

STORY BEHIND THE PHOTO

This memorable encounter took place just after Easter 2013. Kelly and I were travelling along the Brand Highway past the northern outskirts of Perth at around midday, to release a Squelching Froglet (*Crinia insignifera*) at the site where it was found the previous night. It was partly overcast and the temperature was in the mid-twenties.

Parking by the roadside near Gin Gin Brook, I crossed bridge on my way to release the froglet. As I peered into the tannin-stained water, I could make out sub-surface movement from a long and sinuous form near the far bank. The yellow bands were off track for an eel and to my surprise it turned out a magnificent Western Tiger Snake.

I asked Kelly to don her pair of polarisers and stand on the bridge on snake watch. I hurriedly turned the car around and drove down a track leading down to the pool. Fully clothed, I scrambling into the water and began following the instructions from above. I trod slowly and lightly to thwart any excessive clouding of the water. I could make out the snake heading towards the opposite bank and once within range I launched, seizing the tail base and reversing towards land as the fireworks began. It was stocky, muscular and a little over 4ft long in the old scale. Kelly was waiting bankside with the hoop bag and the snake was safely secured and briefly left to dry out and hopefully relax prior to the pending shoot.

I went across and released the little froglet, still reflecting on my luck. I would never have seen the snake in the first place if I was not afforded that vantage point. We set up the 240-volt unleaded generator and ran the lead to power my studio lighting kit, positioning them on a gently sloping embankment with a black sheet as a backdrop. I had a feeling that the greens from the foliage, the brownish clay soils on the embankment and the vibrant yellows on the subject would offer a tasty palette against the black once illuminated by the strobes. I tripod mounted my bellows system coupled to my treasured Leitz 100mm Macro Bellows lens from the seventies and took some exposure shots, varying the output of each studio light until I had a well-exposed scene on which to commence. Still soaked, it took only 20 minutes to prepare the well-rehearsed procedure.

The tiger was gently coaxed into a hide box and after a few failed attempts it settled down sufficiently to allow me to achieve a precise focus and fire off several shots with the head raised. We were in awe of this spectacular snake and the vision of it gliding into the undergrowth following this brief encounter will never be forgotten. I am so grateful for this opportunity. As a photographer, it does not get much better than this. Oh, and the colour palette rocked!

PHOTOGRAPHIC EQUIPMENT USED

Canon EOS 5D Mark III DSLR, vintage Leica Bellows Rail System with third-party Leitax adapter. 100mm Leitz Wetzlar Macro Elmar short lens. Benro tripod, black sheet, Elinchrom Skyport Transmitter hotshoe mounted, Elinchrom DLite4IT Studio Strobes, Yamaha 240v unleaded portable generator, 240v electrical lead.

SPECIES

Inland Taipan (*Oxyuranus microlepidotus*)

PHOTOGRAPHER

Shane Black

STATUS

EX   EW   CR   EN   VU   NT   **LC**

LOCATION

Moon Plain, Coober Pedy, South Australia

NOTES

Total length 2.5m. Also known as the Fierce Snake. Often claimed to be the world's most venomous snake, although it is not the most dangerous as it is shy and encounters with humans are far rarer compared to its relative, the Coastal Taipan. Distributed in remote and arid regions of south-western Queenland and north-eastern South Australia, where inhabits deeply cracked clays of floodplains. Feed exclusively on small mammals in the wild, particularly favouring the Long-haired Rat (*Rattus villosissimus*). Primarily diurnal and most active in the early mornings before retiring into the soil cracks in the heat of the day.

STORY BEHIND THE PHOTO

Having travelled thousands of kilometres across the country to find this species, the anticipation was high when I reached the Moon Plain of South Australia in early October 2017. Unfortunately I arrived to find unseasonably cold weather in the region. The first three days of searching resulted in very little in the way of reptiles. However, the temperature was expected to rise considerably on the fourth day, so I stuck around enduring the cold wet days and nights. On the fourth morning I awoke to clear skies and a warmer day as expected. I rolled the swag up and headed off early hoping for something special.

I wasn't disappointed. At roughly 9am, while driving slowly through the black soil plains, I spotted an adult female Inland Taipan enjoying the morning sun. I was able to approach fairly closely before the snake showed signs of being irritated by my presence. Contrary to most literature, I've found this species to defend itself quite vigorously when annoyed, showing typical taipan defensive behaviour such as dropping its lower jaw exposing its fangs, and flattening of the head. Nevertheless, if shown respect these snakes respond well.

For this image I chose a wide-angle lens to try and capture the arid and remote nature of the country this snake calls home. I was keen to get an image that would sum up this species, and whilst I'm always critical of every photograph I take, with the time restraints I had placed upon myself, I walked away satisfied I had done enough.

I had waited years to find this species in the wild, and it was one of the most treasured experiences in my herping life. I could have spent the whole day with this animal, just watching it and admiring it, but my travelling partner was in a rush to keep moving north. So sadly, I had to eventually let go and walk away. Fittingly, my last view of this snake was it disappearing down a deep crack in the soil.

PHOTOGRAPHIC EQUIPMENT USED

Nikon D800, Nikkor 24mm 2.8D lens, a touch of fill flash, f13, 1/250s, ISO 100.

SPECIES

Coastal Taipan (*Oxyuranus scutellatus*)

PHOTOGRAPHER

Michael Cermak

STATUS

EX   EW   CR   EN   VU   NT   **LC**

LOCATION

Cairns, north Queensland

NOTES

Total length 3m. Alternative name Eastern Taipan. Often regarded as the most dangerous snake in Australia, and has the longest fangs of all Australian elapids at up to 1.2cm. The name 'Taipan' was given to the species by the Wik-Mungkan people of Cape York. Inhabits coastal regions from northern New South Wales, through Queensland and Northern Territory, and into Western Australia. Primarily active during the day, although may become nocturnal in hot weather. Feeds only on warm-blooded prey such as mammals and birds. Hunts using keen eyesight, often with head raised above low-lying vegetation. Once prey is spotted the snake will lunge forward, executing multiple rapid envenomations.

STORY BEHIND THE PHOTO

Shortly after moving to Cairns permanently in 1978, my friend Peter Krauss gave me a taipan that he'd bred. It was a beautiful little 'live wire' hatchling with a white head and pale orange dorsal scales. It ate, pooped and sloughed and grew to 1.5m in its first year as taipans do. I never trust taipan hatchlings or very young juveniles – they are like teenagers, testing and challenging big people, but they usually settle down and become quite docile as adults. However, there are exceptions and Lyall Naylor, my ex-colleague from the zoo, would confirm that.

Anyway, my taipan (I have to apologise to all the pet keepers, I never gave names to my reptiles) grew into a magnificent male probably exceeding 1.8m, although I never measured him. In the 1980s I moved my private collection to the Cairns Tropical Zoo (formally Wild World) where I continued to look after my animals for the following six years. At about this time I started getting more serious about photography and there wasn't a day at work when I wouldn't shoot something or other, of course all on slide film.

One day I was cleaning the taipan enclosure and my boy was sitting on a high log watching every move I made with his sharp eye. It was his eye, in line with my eyes, that inspired me to reach out for the camera. I slowly closed the back door to the enclosure and went to get my camera, hoping that the taipan would be still in the same position. Although the enclosure was quite spacious, there wasn't much room for a shot against suitable background. I opened the door and there he was, looking at me, perfectly calm but that eye had a sign in it saying 'don't mess with me.'

I only took one shot, after which he slid away into the safe place under a log. It wasn't until the box of slides arrived back from Kodak, and I had a chance to take a good look at this image, that I realised how lucky I was. Shooting with a fully manual camera and manually calculated flash output didn't always work out as expected but this time it did.

PHOTOGRAPHIC EQUIPMENT USED

Canon F1, Canon FD50mm lens, Sunpak flashgun, Kodachrome 64.

SPECIES

Western Desert Taipan (*Oxyuranus temporalis*)

PHOTOGRAPHER

Max Jackson

STATUS

 EX EW CR EN VU NT **LC**

LOCATION

Western Deserts, Western Australia

NOTES

Total length 1.7m. Also known as Central Ranges Taipan. Expected to be dangerously venomous. Inhabits the deserts of central eastern Western Australia and south-western Northern Territory. Feeds primarily on mammals. This species wasn't discovered until 2006. It differs from its relatives – the Coastal Taipan (*O. scutellatus*) and Inland Taipan (*O. microlepidotus*) – by having six infralabial scales rather than seven and lacking a temporolabial scale. Because of their dangerous venom, Adelaide Zoo has made an effective antivenin for humans.

STORY BEHIND THE PHOTO

No genus in Australia has a more infamous reputation than the taipans. Although two of its species are extremely well known, the third is considerably more cryptic. Officially described in 2007, there had only been a handful of individuals recorded when a friend and I set out into its extremely remote habitat in January 2016.

Once within the snake's range we only had three days up our sleeve so we weren't overly optimistic at our chances of seeing such a poorly known species. Our plan of attack was to spend every minute from sunrise to sunset cruising the 4WD tracks and hope that luck was on our side. Thankfully it was!

The very first morning I set out in my vehicle at 4.50am and I couldn't believe my eyes when only 15 minutes later I saw this individual – 1.1m in length – crossing the dirt track just as the sun came over the horizon. This is hands down my favourite species that I have ever come across and I was extremely thankful to walk away from the encounter with a shot that I was happy with.

PHOTOGRAPHIC EQUIPMENT USED

Canon 7D, Tokina 11–16mm, Twin Flash Canon EX 480, f16, 1/250s, ISO 160, 16mm. Edited in Lightroom.

SPECIES

Collett's Snake (*Pseudechis colletti*)

PHOTOGRAPHER

Ross McGibbon

STATUS

EX EW CR EN VU NT **LC**

LOCATION

Mitchell Grass Downs, inland Queensland

NOTES

Total length 1.5m. One of Australia's most beautifully coloured snakes. Dangerously venomous. Inhabits black soils of monsoonal flood plains.

STORY BEHIND THE PHOTO

This rare and beautiful snake inhabits a relatively small area of the Mitchell Grass Downs region of inland Queensland and lives exclusively in black soil habitat. Due to the scarcity of rain, the black soil becomes extremely dry, allowing cracks to form deep into the ground. These cracks shelter the snakes from the extreme heat and cold. In the warmer months, they emerge to hunt between dusk and dawn when the surface temperature is tolerable.

Finding one of these elusive snakes in the wild had been one of my dreams for many years. I decided to attempt it in March 2018 with good mates Dan Bromley, Richie Gilbert and Steve Tuckey. To increase our chances of success, we collectively studied as much information as we could about the habitat, habits and distribution of this species. We were surprised to learn that some people had visited the area in search of this snake more than 20 times without success. To make things worse, the region was suffering from extreme drought. The odds were against us.

By February, all our flights, leave and travel plans were locked-in and all we could do now was wait and pray for good weather. Two weeks out, a cyclone formed in the Gulf and tracked south towards Collett's country. This was the miracle rain we were hoping for, but soon we were stressing that it would be too wet as the area received record rainfall and there was widespread flooding. Luckily, by the time we arrived, the rain had cleared and the water had subsided enough for us to commence our search. We scoured the area surrounding Winton, Queensland, for three days with little success. We made the call to move on to our next location a few hours' drive to the north-west and arrived there just before sunset. The road was littered with Eyrean Earless Dragons (*Tympanocryptis tetraporophora*), as well as a few Centralian Blue-tongues (*Tiliqua multifasciata*) and Downs Bearded Dragons (*Pogona henrylawsoni*). It was evident that the area had received the perfect amount of rain to stimulate the wildlife and, with the temperature still hovering around 30°C that evening, we had a feeling that we were in for a good night. As the sun set, we came across our first snake of the evening foraging along the grass lining the road. To our disbelief it was what we had come all this way for – the rare and regal Collett's Snake. We moved it off the road for obvious safety reasons and I asked the guys if I could photograph it first as I wanted to attempt to capture some of the remaining colour in the sky.

The snake started out quite defensively (as black snakes do) but as conditions got darker it was unable to see me very well. It relaxed and began to sit perfectly still, so I took this rare opportunity to attempt a long-exposure shot. With the shutter speed slowed down a little, I was able to capture the element of dusk in the sky and tell the story of the time of day the snake became active. To date, this is one of the most technical photographs I've taken. I still look at this image with disbelief that we even found this snake, let alone photographed it this way.

PHOTOGRAPHIC EQUIPMENT USED

Canon 5D Mark III fitted with an external flash trigger. Tamron 15–30mm wide-angle lens. External speedlight flash fitted with flash receiver and diffuser. Post processing using Adobe Lightroom.

SPECIES

Spotted Black Snake (*Pseudechis guttatus*)

PHOTOGRAPHER

Jason Luke

STATUS

EX　EW　CR　EN　VU　NT　**LC**

LOCATION

Pilliga Nature Reserve, New South Wales

NOTES

Total length 1.5m. Also known as Blue-bellied Black Snake, and often confused with its relative the Red-bellied Black Snake. Occurs in a variety of habitats from swamps to dry sclerophyll forests. Feeds on a wide range of prey, including frogs, lizards and mammals. Dangerously venomous but quite shy in behaviour unless threatened. When defensive will hiss loudly and flatten the body, holding it low to the ground in an S shape.

STORY BEHIND THE PHOTO

I was not overly familiar with the Spotted Black Snake. Although they are common over most of their range, I had not travelled a lot within that area. They were one of my target species to photograph on a recent road trip I did with some friends in January 2019. Conditions on the trip were extremely hot and dry and snakes were scarce. We had found numerous road-killed Spotted Black Snakes on our way up to Queensland. We also found one nice specimen in Queensland, but the immediate habitat it was located in wasn't ideal for the type of shot I was after, so I passed it up.

On the way back to Sydney we had one night in the Pilliga. The temperature was insanely high and our expectations low. On the way to the campsite during the day we passed a large dam full of water so we checked it out. There was plenty of wildlife around it – emus and wallabies reluctantly moved off on our approach, and a large adult Lace Monitor (*Varanus varius*) scuttled up a tree at the edge of the dam. It looked like a good place to come back to at night. We continued back to the campsite and, trying to stay out of the heat, set up our swags and waited for nightfall. Temperatures were in the mid-forties by day and night temperatures were not forecast to drop a great deal. We weren't expecting much.

As dusk came we headed off to the dam and on arrival immediately found an Eastern Stone Gecko (*Diplodactylus vittatus*). That gave us hope that we might see a few things around the dam. We walked down to the water's edge and a Spotted Black Snake was seen within seconds. We photographed the snake using a small log as a backdrop. I used an on-camera speed light (1/1) with a soft box and second lens-mounted screen diffuser and a second mini tripod-mounted remote speed light (1/2) with soft box set to light the background. I particularly like how the large black scales show an armoured look and how light refection on the snake's head highlights the contours of its venom glands, making it look like one tough snake. The dust on the snake's body reminds me of the harsh habitat and conditions this snake endures. We didn't find any other snakes that night, just a few frog and gecko species, but I was very happy to have finally taken a good photo of a Spotted Black Snake.

PHOTOGRAPHIC EQUIPMENT USED

Nikon D800, Sigma 24mm ART f/1.4, 2x Nikon SB910 Speedlights with Lastolight soft boxes and Interfit Strobies Diffuser, Promaster mini tripod, f16, 1/200s, ISO 400, 24mm. Image adjusted on iPhoto.

SPECIES

Red-bellied Black Snake (*Pseudechis porphyriacus*)

PHOTOGRAPHER

Ken Griffiths

STATUS

EX EW CR EN VU NT **LC**

LOCATION

Sydney, New South Wales

NOTES

Total length 1.8m. Dangerously venomous but tends to be inoffensive in nature. Often in wetland habitats – primarily streams, lagoons and swamps – but can be found well away from these areas. Also favours disturbed environments such as agricultural lands. Shelters in areas of thick grass, under logs or in animal burrows. Adults frequent specific shelter locations in their home range. Feeds on vertebrates such as fish, frogs, tadpoles, snakes, lizards and mammals. Hunts widely through water or by climbing several metres, and will swallow prey while still submerged. When fleeing from predators, can stay submerged for as long as 23 minutes. During courtship, the male will approach the female by stroking his chin along her body. To indicate receptivity, she will stretch out, which allows the male to align with her for mating.

STORY BEHIND THE PHOTO

For many years I did wildlife rescues in my area with WIRES and AWARE. This included everything from possums to echidnas and of course reptiles. Red-bellied Blacks were by far the most common snake that set up home in people's yards. Sometimes it was as easy as walking into the property, picking up the snake and dropping into a bag. Other times it required a lot of moving rubbish or ratting around through cluttered garages and garden sheds. The snake pictured here was a little more cunning than most and set up home in a retaining wall. It was very wary and slithered back into the wall at the first hint of any danger.

I made up what I called a snake trap, designed along the lines of a poddy mullet trap, and it was successful on some occasions. I used this for locations that were not too far from home as I baited the trap with a live mouse, enclosed separately so when the snake entered the trap it could not get at the mouse. On this occasion I set the trap up near the entrance to the hole where the snake mostly came from. I placed some towels over the trap and the hole in the wall which essentially provided a path directly to the trap entrance. I told the homeowner that I would return later in the day but she rang me within half an hour and said that the snake was in the trap.

I usually photograph any animals that I release and on this occasion the snake had recently sloughed and had a lot more colouration than normal, making it an ideal photographic specimen. I found a suitable release site, which is always at least 5km away from where the animal was caught, as they can and do return to the same location if released too close to their home range. I usually hold animal releases early or late in the day, depending on the species. This snake was held overnight and the early morning provided cooler temperatures and sunlight. There had been some recent rain and I thought the snake might look good with some reflections in a shallow puddle. The snake was fairly docile and allowed for a few easy photographs before slithering off into the bush.

PHOTOGRAPHIC EQUIPMENT USED

Canon 40D, Canon 70-200F4L, f6.7, 1/350s, ISO 200. Some minor editing in Adobe Photoshop CS6.

SPECIES

Strap-snouted Brown Snake (*Pseudonaja aspidorhyncha*)

PHOTOGRAPHER

Ken Griffiths

STATUS

EX   EW   CR   EN   VU   NT   **LC**

LOCATION

Between Hungerford and Eulo, Queensland

NOTES

Total length 1.5m. Dangerously venomous. Close examination (not recommended!) usually required for positively identification as distribution overlaps with other species of *Pseudonaja*. Pupil can have a reddish-orange ring around it while eye itself is large with dark iris. Has keen eyesight and quick to notice any movement of potential prey. Diurnal hunter, feeding on a wide range of vertebrates including mammals, fledgling birds, other snakes and lizards. Juvenile snakes in captivity prefer small lizards, moving onto rodents once mature. Does not rely solely on venom when hunting – also uses constriction to help kill prey. Predated by Mulga Snakes (*Pseudechis australis*) and birds of prey.

STORY BEHIND THE PHOTO

It was back in 2005 and I was heading off with a couple of mates to western Queensland to do some herp photography. We set off early in the morning from our camp near Hungerford as this was the best part of the day to see reptiles and other wildlife before the heat forces most of them to lay low until the later part of the day. It was a sunny day and the temperature was already in the mid-twenties.

We were not long out when a long, thinnish snake crossed the road just ahead of us. Luckily I managed to avoid running it over and quickly pulled the car to a stop. We managed to coax it into a hoop bag – a safer way to handle dangerous snakes – and walked it a hundred metres or so into the bush where we could try to set it up for a few photographs. We tipped the snake out of the bag and it immediately sat up in a defensive pose and provided us with some nice photo opportunities.

It is not always this easy and we thought ourselves lucky to have made this lovely find. It is such a shame to see so many reptiles dead on our roads – hopefully this guy kept on going in the opposite direction.

PHOTOGRAPHIC EQUIPMENT USED

Canon 20D, 100mm f2.8 macro lens, f13, 1/250s, ISO 100. Minor adjustments in Adobe Photoshop CS6.

SPECIES

Ingram's Brown Snake (*Pseudonaja ingrami*)

PHOTOGRAPHER

Gary Stephenson

STATUS

EX   EW   CR   EN   VU   NT   **LC**

LOCATION

Camooweal, Barkly Tableland, Queensland

NOTES

Total length 1.2m. Dangerously venomous. When agitated known to raise forebody and flatten neck to form a hood. Inhabits low-lying seasonally flooded habitats, sheltering in deep soil cracks when dry.

STORY BEHIND THE PHOTO

Over the past 15 years energy companies in Australia have been exploiting our natural gas reserves. After gas is discovered, production wells are drilled and gas extracted and separated from the associated water. The gas is compressed and transported in pipelines to purification plants.

The sinking of production wells and the construction of pipelines is governed by an Environmental Impact Statement (EIS). The EIS will require the use of fauna-spotters/-catchers, known in the vernacular as 'critter-catchers'. Part of a critter-catcher's role is to initially conduct a pre-construction inspection of a well site or planned route for a pipeline, remove any fauna and keep detailed and accurate records of where the fauna was found and where it was relocated.

During the construction phase where wells are sunk or pipeline trenches are dug, it's common for fauna to fall into these, particularly after dark when daytime temperatures are reaching 50°C.

The Northern Gas Pipeline commenced construction in mid-2017, linking gas wells from the vicinity of Tennant Creek, Northern Territory, to the gas purification plants in Mount Isa, Queensland. The country that this pipeline traverses is largely a semi-arid almost treeless savannah dominated by Mitchell Grass Downs with some occasional sand ridges, usually dry rivers and gorges.

Using traditional methods for locating the specialised reptiles that inhabit the Mitchell Grass Downs is difficult. What is notable in this sun-baked environment is that the heavy reddish-brown (ashy downs) to black clay soil types are deeply cracking. It is down these deep cracks where reptiles will quickly escape once disturbed.

During November and December 2017 I was employed on the Northern Gas Pipeline as a critter-catcher. The day would start with an early-morning inspection of the trench prior to pipes being laid. It was during one of these inspections that this Ingram's Brown Snake was encountered. It was approximately 1.2m in length and was sufficiently warmed in the morning sunlight that it was not about to go willingly into the hoop bag as a first step towards its relocation.

Such bravado deserved some photographs to be taken. This image captures the snake moving forward, after an initial 'looping' strike, with its mouth wide open showing off the bluish-black buccal cavity typical of this species and the closely related Speckled Brown Snake (*Pseudonaja guttata*), another 'black-soil' specialist, which in this location is diagnostic for separating these from other members of the genus.

Taking these types of images is not without risk and a bite to the hand, or worse the face, could lead to an undesirable outcome. Having another competent critter-catcher with you in these circumstances is a must.

PHOTOGRAPHIC EQUIPMENT USED

Nikon D7200, Nikkor 18–200mm 3.5–5.6 G ED zoom lens at 200mm, f18, 1/250sec, ISO 200. Camera-mounted Nikon Speedlight SB-600 on manual setting at ½ power with a circular diffuser and two additional speedlights mounted at right angles above the subject.

SPECIES

Western Brown Snake (*Pseudonaja mengdeni*)

PHOTOGRAPHER

Jari Cornelis

STATUS

EX   EW   CR   EN   VU   NT   **LC**

LOCATION

Ilkurlka, Western Australia

NOTES

Total length 2m. Slender and long in physique and from above has a rounded snout. Scales semi-glossy and smooth. Two distinct morphs of 'orange with black head' and 'pale head, grey nape'. Found across a range of semiarid to arid environments including shrubland, savannah woodlands, grasslands and dry sclerophyll forests. Regarded as dangerously venomous. In a good season females may produce two clutches of up to 38 eggs but on average about 12. Often shelters under fallen timber, rock slabs or corrugated iron sheets, and noted to use abandoned animal burrows. Males in captivity have often been observed in combat, plaiting their bodies together while struggling to pin the opponent's head, and biting has also been recorded, which is unusual.

STORY BEHIND THE PHOTO

I took this image on 14 January 2019 in one of the most remote parts of the world. The heart of the Great Victoria Desert is the most pristine ecosystem I have experienced in my entire life. The lack of people visiting this area is why it is still so beautiful, and aside from the occasional abandoned car from four wheel drive enthusiasts who were underequipped or had an accident there was almost no trace of human activity.

On the way into Ilkurlka, every once in a while we came across a checkpoint with a little logbook and we were the first people to pass that way for weeks. Once we arrived at Ilkurlka and were looking for our target species we found more large elapids than we had ever done before, including Western Browns and Mulga Snakes (*Pseudechis australis*). After a couple of days of searching and not finding our target we came across another Mulga crossing the road and we took a minute to decide whether we were going to photograph it or keep going. At this point it was about midnight but it was so hot that the normally diurnal snakes had no choice but to be active at this time. My friend Elliot and I decided "we might as well," and while Elliot was flat on the floor taking pictures, the most beautiful Western Brown we had seen just sneaked up next to him to check out what we're doing. We had two highly venomous snakes within a metre of us and for a second we didn't really know what to do because we didn't want to lose either of them. The Mulga was pretty relaxed and was just sitting still so we managed to keep an eye on that one while trying to keep the Western Brown from disappearing into the spinifex until it realised that we weren't going to harm it and could manage to get it to sit still long enough to get photos of it.

PHOTOGRAPHIC EQUIPMENT USED

Canon 700D with EF-S 10–18mm f/4.5-5.6 IS STM. Lightroom used for post-processing.

SPECIES

Ringed Brown Snake (*Pseudonaja modesta*)

PHOTOGRAPHER

Jari Cornelis

STATUS

EX EW CR EN VU NT **LC**

LOCATION

Anne Beadell Highway, South Australia

NOTES

Total length 50cm. Described as three species from three specimens in the late 19th century – *Cacophis modesta* from north-western Australia, *Brachysoma sutherlandi* from Carl Creek in north-west Queensland, and *Furina ramsayi* from Milparinka in New South Wales. Once it was realised that all three were the same species the name was changed to *Pseudonaja modesta*, with 'modesta' meaning 'unassuming' or 'well-behaved'. Found living among spinifex in arid shrubland and grassland across inland Australia. Diurnal and feeds predominately on skinks and occasionally small mammals. Listed as dangerously venomous, although in 1987 a girl was reported to have been bitten and suffered mild symptoms but no coagulopathy.

STORY BEHIND THE PHOTO

This photo was taken on 16 January 2019 along the most beautiful road in Australia – the Anne Beadell Highway. Following the heart-breaking decision to give up our search for the Western Desert Taipan (*Oxyuranus temporalis*), we took on the challenge of one of the toughest four wheel drive tracks in Australia and drove from Ilkurlka to Coober Pedy. We fuelled up as much as we could carry from the Ilkurlka Roadhouse ($3 per litre of diesel) and set off on the best drive of the entire ten-week journey. Google Maps told us it would take 33 hours of just driving to reach Coober Pedy, but we ended up taking only 18, not including time for photographing animals and one night of sleeping which was a luxury after barely having slept for four days.

As we crossed the border into South Australia the track was less well maintained and the going started to get tougher. While the sun was setting we started seeing a lot more camels and an old mate manning the roadhouse at Ilkurlka warned us that when the camels get startled they run in front of the car following the dirt track and it can take a while to get past them. We got stuck behind the herd of camels for a whole hour before they realised they could just move off the road and stop running. This was very frustrating because we wanted to get as far as possible towards Coober Pedy and look for our next target. However, soon after we left the camels behind the sun had fully set and a beautiful juvenile Ringed Brown Snake slithered across the road – another new species for me. This little snake, although it has quite a mild venom for a brown snake, was not keen on being photographed so it took a lot of patience for us to get photos we were satisfied with.

PHOTOGRAPHIC EQUIPMENT USED

Canon 700D with EF-S 10-18mm f/4.5-5.6 IS STM. Lightroom used for post-processing.

SPECIES

Eastern Brown Snake (*Pseudonaja textilis*)

PHOTOGRAPHER

Benjamin Stubbs

STATUS

EX EW CR EN VU NT **LC**

LOCATION

Doreen, Victoria

NOTES

Total length 2m. Dangerously venomous. Wide ranging and occurs in woodlands, scrublands and savanna grasslands. Commonly seen suburban periphery areas. Population in southern and eastern New Guinea once considered to have been introduced by humans, but genetic mapping now suggests that it started from individuals that arrived from northern Queensland and Arnhem Land around the Pleistocene. Varied diet of frogs, reptiles, birds and mammals, with smaller individuals eating proportionally more ectothermic prey than larger individuals. Has shown cannibalistic behaviour in captivity.

STORY BEHIND THE PHOTO

I captured this image in mid-afternoon on 21 June 2018. The middle of winter can be slow time for reptiles in Melbourne, but with a little effort our local species can be found under rocks, logs, rubbish and other debris. On this particular day a friend and I had little success but were rewarded near the end of our excursion when this juvenile Eastern Brown Snake was located under a small rock on a steep rocky slope that caught the majority of the sun throughout the day.

We positioned the little snake on a rock with the intention of it sitting quietly in the sun for a quick few photos before we guided it back under its rock. The snake had different ideas, though, and as you can see from the image it was very intent on showing how big and tough it was, being less than co-operative for the entire time.

This was one of the first times I had attempted to photograph a venomous snake with a wide-angle lens, and the short working distances and a small and lively snake made this all the more difficult. I do remember reviewing this image in what was a quick series of shots as this snake moved towards me, and showing it to my friend with a look of glee on my face. I wasn't that happy with the overall composition of the shot, but the snake's behaviour made up for that.

I always look back at this shot with a bit of a smile. Although I know that this image depicts a snake exhibiting defensive behaviour, I can't help but imagine that it is actually laughing about some joke or story it has just overheard. I will always love photographing juvenile brown snakes – such attitude, and if you're lucky very spectacular orange spots or lovely banding as in this particular individual.

PHOTOGRAPHIC EQUIPMENT USED

Nikon D7500, Tamron 10–24 F/3.5-4.5 Di II VC, Nikon Sb-700 Speedlight through 40cm soft box. Minor lighting adjustments made in Adobe Lightroom.

SPECIES

West Coast Banded Snake (*Simoselaps littoralis*)

PHOTOGRAPHER

Jari Cornelis

STATUS

EX EW CR EN VU NT **LC**

LOCATION

Cervantes, Western Australia

NOTES

Snout-vent length up to 25cm. Front fanged and has mild venom. A skilled burrowing species that lives in the pale dunes and limestones of the coast. Typically lays four eggs per clutch and seeks shelter under tussocks, shrubs and leaf litter. Feeds exclusively on lizards.

STORY BEHIND THE PHOTO

This photo was taken on 14 December 2018 on a cold, windy night on the west coast. After a week of dust and heat we felt a bit relieved to be along the coast again, although as soon as I stepped onto the beach and felt how cold the water and the breeze were, I got a bit worried about how many reptiles we would see. This part of the trip was the least organised because we reached the coast a little sooner than anticipated and I was scrambling to find a spot to go herping for the next few nights. I talked to some herpers who'd helped me with locations before and they told me a few roads around Jurien Bay that could be productive, but perhaps a bit hit and miss due to the weather.

We started driving just as the sun was setting and were surprised to find geckos walking around on the road before it was dark, and this gave me a bit of hope. As soon as the sun fully set, we found four snakes within no time, including this beautiful West Coast Banded Snake. I try to photograph animals as naturally as possible within their habitat and that can be tricky with burrowing snakes because they are mainly only found above ground when crossing the road, and when taking pictures on soft sand they can disappear quite easily. Lucky for me this individual didn't try to dig itself into the sand and I was able to capture it on the sand dunes where it usually travels underground. The road where I found this cute little snake was a busy highway where I had to compete with cars driving at 110km per hour and try to help animals off the road. Unfortunately for many I was too late and they had already been run over, including individuals of species I had never seen before.

PHOTOGRAPHIC EQUIPMENT USED

Canon 700D with EF-S 10–18mm f/4.5-5.6 IS STM. Lightroom used for post-processing.

SPECIES

Rough-scaled Snake (*Tropidechis carinatus*)

PHOTOGRAPHER

Ross McGibbon

STATUS

EX EW CR EN VU NT **LC**

LOCATION

Julatten, Queensland

NOTES

Total length 1m. Dull brown with blotches or bands along body. Dangerously venomous and is a ready biter – venom strongly neurotoxic and is responsible for at least one human death and several envenomations. Feeds mainly on mammals and frogs, sometimes also birds and lizards. Looks similar to the non-venomous Keelback (*Tropidonophis mairii*), and the two species share range and habitat.

STORY BEHIND THE PHOTO

In April 2018, my good mate Dan and I were rounding off a three-week herping trip around Queensland with a few days in north Queensland. The first thing on our agenda was to meet up with our mates Shane and Steve for a few days of herping around Mount Molloy and Julatten, north of Cairns. As it was already getting late in the afternoon, we made our way to some rainforest habitat near Julatten where, after sundown, we aimed to locate an impressive species of reptile called the Chameleon Gecko.

Shane and Steve led the way while Dan and I followed in the car behind. As the bitumen road gave way to a dirt track we crossed a small bridge over a creek. On the other side we noticed Shane swerve at the last minute to straddle a stick in the middle of the track. Dan and I were following quite close and did the same correction to straddle the stick but Dan said: "Hang on, was that a snake?" We stopped and walked back to the stick/snake only to see a stunning, 80cm-long Rough-scaled Snake sitting dead still in the middle of the track. Luckily it was unharmed and we phoned the guys to come back.

On Shane and Steve's return we all had a laugh about how it becomes second nature for herpers to swerve around sticks on the road on the off chance it is a snake. This time our reactions had paid off. I was extremely excited about our chance encounter with this beautifully banded Rough-scaled Snake, as the specimens up here are far more attractive than the ones I was used to seeing further south on the Sunshine Coast.

We repositioned it off the track to photograph it as the next car to come along my not be as reactive. Rough-scaled snakes are notorious for having pugnacious temperaments, however the calm disposition of this individual made for an easy shoot. It is experiences like this that continually reinforce just how individual the temperaments of snakes can be, despite what the literature states.

PHOTOGRAPHIC EQUIPMENT USED

Canon 5D Mark III, Tamron 15–30mm wide-angle lens, external speedlight flash and diffuser. Post processing using Adobe Lightroom.

SPECIES

Common Bandy Bandy (*Vermicella annulata*)

PHOTOGRAPHER

Jason Luke

STATUS

EX EW CR EN VU NT **LC**

LOCATION

Heathcote, New South Wales

NOTES

Total length 60cm. A striking snake with 48 or more black and white bands. Burrowing species with nocturnal habits. Usually found under rocks and logs, but on humid nights can be encountered crossing roads. Known for its looping defensive display that is believed to confuse predators and protect its head, which remains on the ground during the display. Venomous, but little is known about the toxicology. One reported incident of a bite that resulted in moderately severe but localised symptoms.

STORY BEHIND THE PHOTO

This is a common snake around the Sydney area, and when conditions suit it's possible to find a few in one night. Despite this, they are still one of my favourite snakes to see and photograph. Their striking pattern, placid nature and unusual 'looping' defence posture always make for an interesting yet easy subject to work with. I particularly like how the diffused light from the soft box details the snake's scales in the black sections of their pattern, although their constant looping changes can make finding that 'perfect pose' a little frustrating, especially when working super close with a 24mm lens.

This particular image was taken just after dusk on 3 January 2019 whilst walking with friends along a track in Heathcote National Park just south of Sydney. The weather leading up to and on the day had been hot and dry with temperatures averaging 30°C, and minimum night temperatures of 21°C. Success in finding snakes in such hot and dry conditions can be sporadic on this track and I prefer the temperature to either be mild or hot with recent rain, although I live by the rule that you'll always find less if you're at home watching TV.

We started the walk late in the afternoon in the hope of seeing some diurnal snake and lizard species, but not much seemed to be active. Just as the light was fading around 6pm I spotted the bandy bandy on the edge of the track. I was surprised to find one so early as I usually come across them much later in the night as they are nocturnal. I decided to photograph it as it was of decent size and in good condition, and was readily doing its looping defence posture. It was photographed on the edge of the track where it was found and a seed pod from *Banksia serrata* was used as a background prop. I used an on-camera speed light (1/1) with a soft box and second lens-mounted screen diffuser and a second mini tripod-mounted remote speed light (1/2) with soft box set to light the background. I didn't find or photograph anything else that night so was happy I'd made the effort to photograph the bandy bandy.

PHOTOGRAPHIC EQUIPMENT USED

Nikon D800, Sigma 24mm ART f/1.4, two Nikon SB910 Speedlights with Lastolight soft boxes and Interfit Strobies Diffuser, Promaster mini tripod, f16, 1/250s, ISO 100, 24mm. Image adjusted using iPhoto.

INDEX

A
Acanthophis antarcticus 222
Acrochordus arafurae 212
Amethystine Python 210
Amphibolurus burnsi 158
Arafura File Snake 212
Aspidites ramsayi 198
Austrelaps ramsayi 224

B
Bell's Turtle 76
Black Mountain Skink 144
Black-eyed Gecko 102
Blue Mountains Water Skink 138
Blue-tailed Skink 130
Boiga irregularis 214
Boyd's Forest Dragon 170
Broad-headed Snake 236
Broad-shelled Long-necked Turtle 58
Brown Tree Snake 214
Burns' Dragon 158

C
Cape York Graceful Tree Frog 22
Carlia longipes 126
Carphodactylus laevis 80
Central Bearded Dragon 178
Central Netted Dragon 164
Central Pygmy Spiny-tailed Skink 132
Centralian Carpet Python 200
Centralian Knob-tailed Gecko 82
Chameleon Gecko 80
Chelodina burrungandjii 56
  longicollis 60
  expansa 58

Chillagoe Litter-skink 148
Chlamydosaurus kingi 160
Clarence River Turtle 68
Closed-litter Rainbow Skink 126
Coastal Taipan 242
Collared Whipsnake 230
Collett's Snake 246
Common Bandy Bandy 266
Common Death Adder 222
Common Scaly-foot 124
Common Tree Snake 216
Concinnia tigrinus 128
Coppertail Whipsnake 226
Coromandel Striped Gecko 94
Crocodylus johnstoni 50
  porosus 52
Cryptoblepharus egeriae 130
Ctenophorus decresii 162
  nuchalis 164
  slateri 166

D
Dainty Green Tree Frog 26
Delma concinna 122
Demansia reticulata cupreiceps 226
  shinei 228
  torquata 230
Dendrelaphis punctulatus 216
Desert Spadefoot 42
Diamond Python 206
Diplodactylus pulcher 90
Dreeite Water Skink 140
Drysdalia coronoides 232
Duvaucel's Gecko 92
Dwarf Bearded Dragon 176

E
Eastern Brown Snake 260
Eastern Dwarf Sedge Frog 24
Eastern Water Dragon 172
Egernia eos 132
  stokesii zellingi 134
Elegant Gecko 106
Elseya dentata 62
  irwini 64
Elusor macrurus 66
Emoia atrocostata 136
Emydura macquarii binjing 68
  tanybaraga 70
  victoriae 72
Eulamprus leuraensis 138
  tympanum marniae 140
  tympanum tympanum 142
Eyre Basin Beaked Gecko 114

F
Fitzroy River Turtle 74
Forest Gecko 100
Freshwater Crocodile 50
Frillneck 160
Fringe-toed Velvet Gecko 112

G
Gidgee Skink 134
Golden-tailed Gecko 118
Great Desert Skink 146
Green and Golden Bell Frog 20
Green Python 208
Gulf Marbled Velvet Gecko 110

H
Harlequin Gecko 120
Heath Frog 28
Heleioporus albopunctatus 40
Highland Copperhead 224
Hoplocephalus bitorquatus 234
  bungaroides 236
Hoplodactylus duvauceli 92

I
Ingram's Brown Snake 254
Inland Taipan 240
Intellagama lesueurii lesueurii 172

J
Javelin Delma 122
Javelin Frog 30

K
Kuranda Tree Frog 32

L
Lace Monitor 196
Lepidodactylus listeri 96
Liburnascincus scirtetis 144
Liopholis kintorei 146
Lister's Gecko 96
Litoria aurea 20
  bella 22
  fallax 24
  gracilenta 26
  littlejohni 28
  micobelos 30
  myola 32
  rothii 34
  spenceri 36
  xanthomera 38

Lophosaurus boydii 170
Lucasium occultum 98
Lycodon capucinus 218
Lygisaurus rococo 148

M

Macleay's Water Snake 220
Macrochelodina expansa 58
Mangrove Monitor 188
Mangrove Skink 136
Mary River Turtle 66
McCann's Skink 150
Mertens' Water Monitor 190
Mitchell's Water Monitor 192
Mokopirirakau granulatus 100
    kahutarae 102
Mokopirirakau sp. 104
Moloch horridus 174
Morelia bredli 200
    carinata 202
    spilota metcalfei 204
    spilota spilota 206
    viridis 208
Murray/Darling Carpet Python 204

N

Naultinus elegans 106
    stellatus 108
Nephrurus amyae 82
    asper 84
    wheeleri wheeleri 86
Northern Leaf-tailed Gecko 88
Northern Red-faced Turtle 72
Northern Snapping Turtle 62
Northern Spiny-tailed Gecko 116
Northern Yellow-faced Turtle 70
Notaden nichollsi 42
Notechis scutatus occidentalis 238

O

Oedura bella 110
    filicipoda 112
Oligosoma maccanni 150
Orange-thighed Tree Frog 38
Oriental Wolf Snake 218
Ornate Burrowing Frog 44
Oxyuranus microlepidotus 240
    scutellatus 242
    temporalis 244

P

Pale-headed Snake 234
Perentie 184
Platyplectrum ornatum 44
    spenceri 46
Pogona minor 176
    vitticeps 178
Pretty Gecko 90
Prickly Knob-tailed Gecko 84
Pseudechis colletti 246
    guttatus 248
    porphyriacus 250
Pseudoferania polylepis 220
Pseudonaja aspidorhyncha 252
    ingrami 254
    mengdeni 256
    modesta 258
    textilis 260
Pygopus lepidopodus 124

R

Red-bellied Black Snake 250
Rheobatrachus silus 48
Rheodytes leukops 74
Rhynchoedura eyrensis 114
Ringed Brown Snake 258
Roth's Tree Frog 34
Rough-scaled Python 202
Rough-scaled Snake 264

Rusty Monitor 194

S

Saltuarius cornutus 88
Saltwater Crocodile 52
Sand Monitor 186
Sandstone Long-necked Turtle 56
Saproscincus basiliscus 152
    mustelinus 154
Saw-shelled Turtle 78
Shine's Whipsnake 228
Shingleback 156
Simalia kinghorni 210
Simoselaps littoralis 262
Slater's Ring-tailed Dragon 166
Smooth-snouted Earless
    Dragon 180
Snake-necked Turtle 60
Southern Banded Knob-tailed
    Gecko 86
Southern Gastric Brooding Frog 48
Southern Water Skink 142
Southern Wet Tropics
    Shadeskink 152
Spencer's Burrowing Frog 46
Sphenodon punctatus 54
Spiny-tailed Monitor 182
Spotted Black Snake 248
Spotted Tree Frog 36
Starred Gecko 108
Strap-snouted Brown Snake 252
Strophurus ciliaris ciliaris 116
    taenicauda 118
Swamplands Lashtail 168

T

Tautuku Gecko 104
Tawny Dragon 162
Thorny Devil 174
Tiliqua rugosa aspera 156
Toropuku 'Coromandel' 94
Tropicagma temporalis 168
Tropidechis carinatus 264
Tuatara 54
Tukutuku rakiurae 120
Tympanocryptis intima 180

V

Varanus acanthurus 182
    giganteus 184
    gouldii gouldii 186
    indicus 188
    mertensi 190
    mitchelli 192
    semiremex 194
    varius 196
Vermicella annulata 266

W

Weasel Skink 154
West Coast Banded Snake 262
Western Brown Snake 256
Western Desert Taipan 244
Western Spotted Frog 40
Western Tiger Snake 238
White-lipped Snake 232
Wollumbinia belli 76
    latisternum 78
Woma 198

Y

Yellow-blotched Forest Skink 128
Yellow-headed Snapping Turtle 64
Yellow-snouted Ground Gecko 98

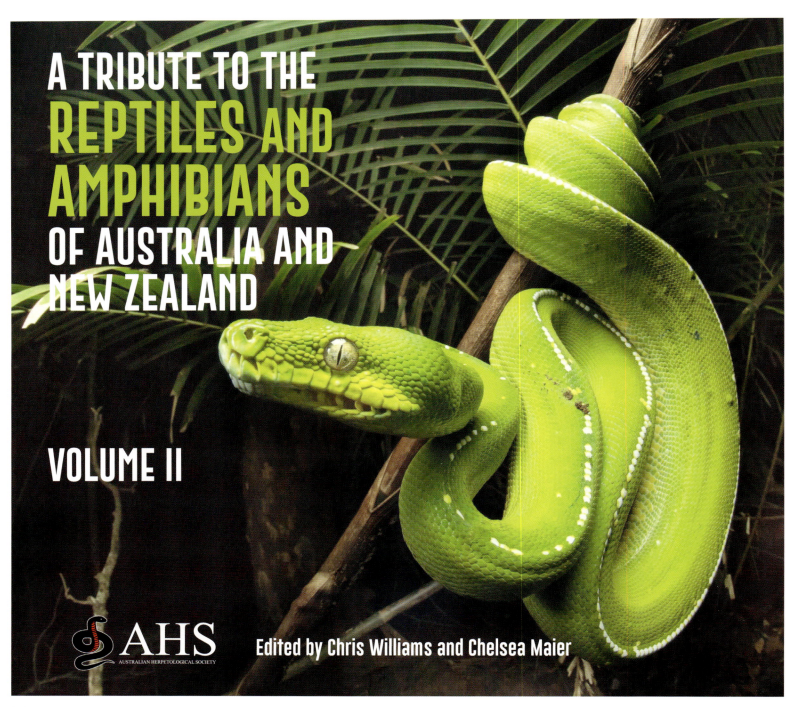

Volume 2 coming soon!

Featuring images from:
- Jasmine Vink • Marion Anstis • Tess Poynter • Sophie Cross
- Chelsea Maier • Jannico Kelk • Lucy Kania • and many more

Submissions are still open for Volume 2. We'd love to be able to showcase five images from talented, yet undiscovered photographers. For more information please email Chelsea Maier at
chelseamaier@gmail.com

ACKNOWLEDGEMENTS

A book like this is only possible with the support and collaboration of a great many people. We owe a huge debt to all 25 contributing photographers, as their support of the project brought it to life. In order to ensure against duplicates, often many more photos were submitted than ended up in these pages.

The Australian Herpetological Society is fortunate to have an active and passionate committee who offered advice on the book's development and photo selection. In particular Bob King, Anthony Tonks, Glenn Shea, Kelly Nowak, Kane Durrant, Rachael Durrant, Mitchell Hodgson, Frank Valckenborgh, Anthony Stimson and Andrew Melrose.

Reptile taxonomy is rapidly changing and Scott Eipper, Steve Wilson and Mitchell Hodgson helped to ensure that all scientific names were correct and current. Any errors are due to the editors.

Hal Cogger was supportive of the project since its inception and graciously agreed to write the foreword.

Thank you to all involved for bringing this publication to fruition. Bring on volume 2!

REFERENCES

Books
Anstis, M. 2017. *Tadpoles and Frogs of Australia* (Second Edition). Reed New Holland.
Cogger, H.G. 2014. *Reptiles and Amphibians of Australia*. CSIRO.
Jewell, T., and Morris, R. 2008. *A Photographic Guide to Reptiles and Amphibians of New Zealand*. Reed New Holland.
Wilson, S., and Swan, G. 2017. *A Complete Guide to Reptiles of Australia* (Fifth Edition). Reed New Holland.

Websites
www.ala.org.au
www.arod.com.au/arod
www.iucnredlist.org
www.livefoods.com.au
www.reptiles.org.nz/herpetofauna/native

Other Natural History titles by Reed New Holland include:

Crocodiles of the World
Colin Stevenson
ISBN 978 1 92554 628 6

A Photographic Guide to Reptiles and Amphibians of New Zealand
Tony Jewell and Rod Morris
ISBN 978 1 86966 203 5

Tadpoles and Frogs of Australia Second Edition
Marion Anstis
ISBN 978 1 92554 601 9

A Complete Guide to Reptiles of Australia Fifth Edition
Steve Wilson and Gerry Swan
ISBN 978 1 92554 602 6

Reed Concise Guide to Snakes of Australia
Gerry Swan
ISBN 978 1 92151 789 1

A Field Guide to Reptiles of Queensland Second Edition
Steve Wilson
ISBN 978 1 92151 748 8

A Field Guide to Reptiles of New South Wales Third Edition
Gerry Swan, Ross Sadlier and Glenn Shea
ISBN 978 1 92554 608 8

World of Reptiles
A photographic celebration of the planet's crocodiles, lizards, snakes, turtles and tuataras
ISBN 978 1 92554 653 8

For details of these books and hundreds of other Natural History titles see
www.newhollandpublishers.com
and follow ReedNewHolland on Facebook and Instagram